METHODS
FOR
POLICY
RESEARCH

Applied Social Research Methods Series
Volume 3

Applied Social Research Methods Series

Series Editor:
LEONARD BICKMAN, Peabody College, Vanderbilt University

Series Associate Editor:
DEBRA ROG, Joint Legislative Audit and
Review Commission, Commonwealth of Virginia

This series is designed to provide students and practicing professionals in the social sciences with relatively inexpensive softcover textbooks describing the major methods used in applied social research. Each text introduces the reader to the state of the art of that particular method and follows step-by-step procedures in its explanation. Each author describes the theory underlying the method to help the student understand the reasons for undertaking certain tasks. Current research is used to support the author's approach. Examples of utilization in a variety of applied fields, as well as sample exercises, are included in the books to aid in classroom use.

Volumes in this series:

1. **SURVEY RESEARCH METHODS,** Floyd J. Fowler, Jr.
2. **THE INTEGRATIVE RESEARCH REVIEW: A Systematic Approach,** Harris M. Cooper
3. **METHODS FOR POLICY RESEARCH,** Ann Majchrzak
4. **SECONDARY RESEARCH: Information Sources and Methods,** David W. Stewart
5. **CASE STUDY RESEARCH: Design and Methods,** Robert K. Yin
6. **META-ANALYTIC PROCEDURES FOR SOCIAL RESEARCH,** Robert Rosenthal

Additional volumes currently in development

METHODS FOR POLICY RESEARCH

Ann Majchrzak

Foreword by AMITAI ETZIONI

Applied Social Research Methods Series
Volume 3

 SAGE PUBLICATIONS Beverly Hills London New Delhi

H
97
.m35
1984

Copyright © 1984 by Sage Publications, Inc.

For information address:

SAGE Publications, Inc.
275 South Beverly Drive
Beverly Hills, California 90212

SAGE Publications India Pvt. Ltd.
C-236 Defence Colony
New Delhi 110 024, India

SAGE Publications Ltd
28 Banner Street
London EC1Y 8QE, England

Printed in the United States of America

Library of Congress Cataloging in Publication Data

Majchrzak, Ann.
　Methods for policy research.
　　(Applied social research methods series ;
　v. 3)
　　Bibliography: p.
　　1. Policy sciences—Research. I. Title. II. Series.
H97.M35　1984　　　361.6'1'072　　　84-9878
ISBN 0-8039-2059-8
ISBN 0-8039-2060-1 (pbk.)

FIRST PRINTING

CONTENTS

Foreword by Amitai Etzioni   7

Preface   9

1   The Nature of Policy Research   11

Policy Research Defined   12
Context of Policy Research   14
Types of Policy Research   15
Characteristics of Policy Research Studies   18
The Policy Research Process   20
Exercises   21

2   Preparing for a Policy Research Study   23

Focus of Information Inquiry   24
Steps to Information Inquiry   32
Decision to Conduct the Study   40
Exercises   42

3   Conceptualizing the Policy Research Study   43

Develop a Preliminary Model of the Social Problem   43
Formulate Specific Research Questions   47
Select Research Investigators   52
Exercises   54

4   Technical Analysis   55

Operationalization of Variables   55
Design of Study Methodology   58
Results and Conclusions   68
Developing Tentative Policy Recommendations   71
Exercises   73

5   Analysis of Study Recommendations   75

Analysis of Implementation Parameters   76
Predict Potential Consequences of Recommendations   83

	Estimating the Probability of Implementation	85
	Preparation of Final Recommendations	86
	Exercises	89
6	**Communicating Policy Research to Policymakers**	**91**
	Guideline 1: Communicate Throughout the Study	92
	Guideline 2: Communicate to Different Users	94
	Guideline 3: Effective Presentation Creates the Basis for Good Communication	95
	Guideline 4: Oral Communication Is Usually More Effective than Written	100
	Closing	101
	Exercises	101
Policy Research Glossary		**103**
References		**105**
About the Author		**111**

FOREWORD

The issue is a very old one indeed. How to bring knowledge to bear on policy decisions? Plato reflected upon it in the terms of his age. His ingenious solution was to unify in one person both analysis and policymaking by crowning a philosopher king. If this solution was practical for a city-polity, I leave it to historians. It will not serve a complex modern society, in which knowledge is mass produced—and policymakers are never knowledge makers, even if this was their specialty before they were elected or appointed to their august offices.

Once one recognizes that two social positions—two specialties, two elites—at work are complementary but not reducible, all the issues Ann Majchrzak deals with (following very much on her own, work we started together) must be faced.

One problem might be called "blue yondering," the danger that the knowledge makers will build knowledge of interest and value to them. (Some campus-based researchers talk about "Robin Hooding" applied funds to advance their basic research.) A parallel problem is that of policymakers who heed not knowledge directly available to them, relevant to their decisions.

Assuming relevant knowledge and an open-minded policymaker, the problems of bridge design arise. In what form is knowledge best transmitted from the knowledge makers to the policymakers? Hefty tomes? Single-spaced, footnoted reprints? Or oral briefing, followed by "eyes-only" memos? (At least one president refused memos longer than one page, and another often asked information to be put on tape, for his T.V. set.)

Least understood—and Ann Majchrzak deserves much credit for stressing this point—is the role of power in the interaction between knowledge makers and policymakers. The same report will have much more of an impact—and in a way ought to —if submitted by a commission which built a wide coalition and consensus on its behalf (e.g., the Social Security Commission) than if submitted merely by a panel of experts. Ideas and data do *not* fly on their own wings. This does not mean that they have no role of their own: Naked power may be as weak as knowledge with backers. The combination works best to bridge knowledge and decision.

In the years to come, resources in both the public and the private sector will continue to be much in demand—that is, scarce. Hence, the commanding need to use them wisely. If Ann Majchrzak's book will get the audience it deserves, there is a fair chance we all will be richer for it.

—Amitai Etzioni
The George Washington University and
Director, Center for Policy Research

PREFACE

Methods for Policy Research was written to help beginning social scientists (at the advanced undergraduate and graduate levels) conduct research in the pursuit of resolving social problems. The social scientists to which this book is addressed may be from any of a number of different disciplines and areas of research interest. He or she could be an organizational behaviorist attempting to increase the effectiveness of public sector social programs, a psychologist interested in reducing the incidence of schizophrenia, a sociologist concerned with urban decay, an educational researcher focused on improving teaching techniques, or a political scientist working on the optimal administrative structure of state governments. The binding element in this book is not the discipline nor the research area, but rather the desire to undertake research that will be used by decisionmakers to help solve today's complex social problems.

This text is a compendium of conceptualizations, suggestions, and examples stemming from years of experience in undertaking policy research efforts. The content and organization of this compendium should make the text a useful reference to any social scientist interested in producing research results useful in the public policy arena. The text consists of six chapters.

Chapter 1: "The Nature of Policy Research" defines policy research and presents several key characteristics of successful policy research efforts.

Chapter 2: "Preparing for a Policy Research Study" describes activities involved in the preparation of a policy research effort, including identifying and defining the research problem, gathering information about resources, and deciding whether or not policy research is appropriate.

Chapter 3: "Conceptualizing the Policy Research Study" offers numerous suggestions for conceptualizing policy research efforts. These suggestions concern the development of a preliminary model of the selected problem, formulating specific research questions, and selecting appropriate research investigators.

Chapter 4: "Technical Analysis" describes the analysis of factors potentially causing the social problem under study. Suggestions are offered about operationalizing variables, designing research methodologies, selecting results and conclusions, and developing tentative recommendations.

Chapter 5: "Analysis of Study Recommendations" presents a detailed procedure for examining policy-relevant variables in order to modify initial policy recommendations to enhance their likelihood of implementation.

Chapter 6: "Communicating Policy Research to Policymakers" discusses the dynamics and importance of communication in the policy research process. Several suggestions for developing an effective communication process between policy researchers and policymakers are presented.

In these six chapters, I hope to alleviate some of the frustrated appeals of those social scientists who feel that their knowledge and experience have not been adequately utilized by policymakers. In addition, by consequence, I hope to respond to those policymakers who have complained about the lack of relevance of social science research in helping to resolve real-world problems.

I wish to thank several people without whom this book would not have been written. First, I wish to acknowledge the substantial contribution of Amitai Etzioni. His comments and suggestions offered while preparing an earlier version of this text were exceedingly helpful, to say the least. In addition, much of the conceptualization of Chapter 5 was derived from conversations I have had with Amitai over the last two years. Second, I thank Pam Doty, a friend and colleague, who has been untiring in her willingness to read and comment on numerous drafts. Despite the aid of Amitai and Pam, the responsibility for the content is entirely mine. Third, I acknowledge the support of the United Nations Fund for Population Activities, which provided the encouragement for teaching the policy research process to others. Finally I thank my husband, Peter Niemiec, for his generous patience and support through it all.

This book is dedicated to my parents, Shirley and Alfred Majchrzak. Without my mother's foresight and intellectual guidance, I would never have tried to help alleviate some of today's social problems. Without my father's sense of reality, my efforts would have been lost in the clouds.

1

The Nature of Policy Research

In this first chapter, policy research is defined, the context of doing research for the policy arena is discussed, types of policy research are presented, and characteristics of policy research studies are described.

Have you ever thought about applying your academic research training to help today's leaders solve real-world problems? In the pages that follow, a research process is described. This process, called *policy research*, is specifically directed at providing policymakers with the options and information they need to solve the problems we face today.

In describing the policy research process, a sequence of activities is outlined that begins with the researcher's preparation for the study and ends with final briefings and recommendations. Although this guide portrays specific steps to be followed by beginning policy researchers, do not let this detailed sequence of activities deceive you! Policy research is more than simply following a set of activities. In the words of Peter Rossi and his colleagues:

> [Policy research] is a mixture of science, craftlore, and art. The science is the body of theory, concepts, and methodological principles; the craftlore, the set of workable techniques, rules of thumb, and standard operating procedures; and art, the pace, style, and manner in which one works. (Rossi, Wright, & Wright, 1978, p. 173)

Implied by this mixture, then, is that "there can no more be only one approved mode of policy research than there can be only one way of learning" (Wildavsky, 1979, p. 281). Activities undertaken in the name of policy research will vary not only with the problem being addressed, but with the style, creativity, and judgment of the researcher. Therefore, this book offers guidelines where it can: It dwells on the "science," provides suggestions for the craftlore, and only hints at the art. The readers are left to contemplate how they would tailor the policy research process to fit their own creative personalities.

Before describing the sequence of activities for conducting policy research studies, it would be helpful to have a better understanding of the nature of policy research. In this first chapter, policy research is defined, the context of doing research for the policy arena is discussed, types of policy research are presented, and characteristics of policy research studies are described. With this background, you will then be ready to learn about the activities involved in doing policy research.

POLICY RESEARCH DEFINED

The following family planning document is an example of policy research.

In response to the Carter Administration's highly vocal opposition to abortion and its search for alternatives, the National Family Planning Forum, Zero Population Growth, and Planned Parenthood Federation of America jointly sponsored a policy research study on the status of family planning in the U.S. in 1977 (Planned Parenthood, 1977). Designed for congressional policymakers, the resulting document not only described the current status of family planning, but also recommended a detailed legislative program to address the remaining problems of unwanted fertility in the U.S. Given the policy relevance of the document as well as the effective lobbying of the sponsors, both the nucleus and legislation for H.R. 11007— the "Comprehensive Family Planning Services, Research in Human Reproduction and Prevention of Unwanted Teenage Pregnancy Act of 1978"—was introduced into the House of Representatives.

As a policy research study, this document has yielded findings that were relevant to the decisionmakers. *Policy research, therefore, is defined as the process of conducting research on, or analysis of, a fundamental social problem in order to provide policymakers with pragmatic, action-oriented recommendations for alleviating the problem.* Stated in a different way, a policy research effort begins with a social problem, such as malnutrition, poverty, or inflation, evolves through a research process whereby alternative policy actions for alleviating the problem are developed, and communicates these alternatives to the policymakers.

Although there are several types of research processes that may affect efforts to alleviate social problems (e.g., applied or basic research), policy research is unique in focusing on *action-oriented* recommendations to *fundamental* social problems. Figure1.1 presents a simplified typology of different research processes.

The figure presents four types of research processes that might affect social problems. These processes are basic research, technical research, policy analysis, and policy research. *Basic social research* refers here to the traditional academic research that is generally done in disciplinary departments of universities. A classic example of basic research are the Asch studies of conformity and consensus in groups. *Technical social research* in-

Focus

		Technical	Fundamental
Action-orientation	Low	Policy Analysis	Basic Research Policy Analysis
	High	Technical Research	Policy Research

Figure 1.1 Research Process Affecting Social Problems

volves projects that are structured to resolve very specific, narrowly defined problems, such as the adequate size of a nuclear power plant or the most appropriate accountability system for social service programs. Questioning whether the power plant should be built or how social service funds should be allocated are not discussed in technical research. The third type of research process, *policy analysis,* is the study of the policymaking process. Policy analysis is typically performed by political scientists interested in the process by which policies are adopted as well as the effects of those policies once adopted.

In Figure 1.1, these four processes have been classified by both their *action orientation* and *focus.* Research processes with high action orientation imply a greater concern for the immediate utility of results than do processes with low action orientation. Research processes may also focus on either technical questions or on fundamental issues (e.g., care of the elderly), with the latter attempting to resolve research questions that are more broadly defined, are multifaceted, and have more diverse consequences for large groups of people.

By the classification scheme of Figure 1.1, policy research has both a high action orientation and a concern for fundamental social problems. Policy research is similar to both basic research and policy analysis as it deals with fundamental social problems. Furthermore, policy research is similar to technical research because of its high action orientation. However, policy research is the only type of research process with an orientation both to action and to fundamental problems. This orientation implies that in an attempt to provide decisionmakers with useful recommendations, all possible actions for resolving fundamental problems are submitted to critical scrutiny. In this way, only those actions that are the most appropriate are recommended.

A final comparison of policy research is worth brief mention. Occasionally, policy research is equated with *evaluation research*. The two should not be confused. Whereas both research processes are concerned with social programs, evaluation research attempts to judge the utility of existing social *programs*. In contrast, a policy research study examines a particular social *problem* and seeks out alternative ways to solve the problem (including, but not limited to, social programs).

In sum, policy research efforts study fundamental social problems in an attempt to create pragmatic courses of action for ameliorating those problems. No other type of research process has quite the same focus or action orientation.

CONTEXT OF POLICY RESEARCH

To do effective policy research involves more than substantive knowledge of a particular subject (e.g., education). Policy research also involves more than an expertise in the application of different methodological and analytical tools. For policy research to yield usable and implementable recommendations, the research process necessitates an understanding of the policymaking arena in which the study results will be received. In this section, relevant aspects of the policymaking arena are briefly described. See such references as Dror (1969), Dye (1978), Jones (1970), Ingram and Mann (1980), Nieman and Lovell (1981) and Woll (1974) for more detailed discussions of the policymaking process in the United States.

A first aspect of the policy arena relevant to policy research is that research findings are only one of many inputs to a policy decision. Other inputs include the views and wishes of constituencies, testimonials, the "give-and-take" of colleagues and superiors, staff opinions, existing policies, and preconceived attitudes. Furthermore, since legislators believe their obligation as policymakers is to create harmony and compromise, "the true does not [necessarily] determine the good" (Brandl, 1980, p. 42). In other words, if the wishes of constituents directly conflict with research recommendations, the research recommendations will not generally be followed. Finally, since there are so many goods, all of which cannot be accomplished, policymakers find that they must always prioritize those goods. Therefore, in understanding any policy research effort, policy researchers need to be able to indicate to the decisionmakers why a recommended action will have greater benefits than all other possible actions.

A second aspect of the policy arena relevant to policy research is that policy is not made, it accumulates. Policymakers typically deal with social problems that are complex, elusive, and not easily resolved. As a result, social problems can only be alleviated through a series of successive approximations in which policies are continually suggested, implemented, evaluated, and revised. Reflecting this process, policy research must be able to provide the empirical evidence to support this series of successive approximations. By supporting this process, policy researchers and policymakers can come to realize that the social sciences do not offer a panacea for social problems; rather, what they can provide is valuable information that may one day help to prevent the occurrence of certain social problems (Campbell, 1969).

A final aspect of the policy arena is that the process of making policies is as complex as the social problem itself. The process is complex, because it is composed of numerous different actors, operating at different policymaking levels and juggling a myriad of different policy mechanisms with different intended and unintended consequences. For example, an effective regulatory change to protect the environment would involve not only Congress, constituencies, the administration, and industry to draft the legislation, but staff at the Environmental Protection Agency and local citizenry to implement the legislation once drafted. Furthermore, whether the legislation is a primarily symbolic one or has the means to enforce compliance in large part will determine the effectiveness of the new policy. Clearly, without at least a general understanding of the policymaking process for a particular issue—including the relevant actors and policy mechanisms—the policy researcher cannot begin to provide decisionmakers with useful information.

In sum, the context of doing policy research consists of competing inputs, complex problems, and seemingly irrational decisionmaking styles. In such a context, policy research seems hardly feasible. Nevertheless, if done properly, with an appreciation for this context, research can provide policymakers with information that will help them with the difficult decisions they face.

TYPES OF POLICY RESEARCH

It has only been within the last decade or so (e.g., with publications by Etzioni, 1971; Horowitz, 1971; Huitt, 1968) that policy research has been identified and discussed as an approach for providing policymakers with relevant information. Despite the recency of its emergence, the attention accorded policy research has been overwhelming, witnessed by the explosive growth in the 1970s of policy research organizations, institutes, journals, and training programs (Robey, 1982). This growth is just beginning to stabilize, allowing time to reflect on such important issues as ethics and standards (Nagel, 1982).

Perhaps due to its explosive growth, or because of the complex nature of its subject, policy research does not describe a singular activity. Policy research efforts vary in whether they have funders who are also study users, the extent to which they focus on problem definition, the organizational context in which they are conducted, and the disciplinary backgrounds of the researchers. Since each of these variations presents important implications for the specific ways in which the policy research process unfolds, a brief discussion of these variations is warranted.

Policy research varies as to whether the funding source is or is not the study user. Policy research may be funded by any number of different sources, such as a government agency (e.g., Department of Labor), interest group or constituency (e.g., Common Cause), or a private philanthropic organization (e.g., Busch or Ford Foundations). For some studies, such as those funded by some foundations, the funding source may not be interested in making direct use of the study results for its own purposes. In such cases, policy researchers are able to study and critique efforts to solve social problems without concern for negative consequences that might result from criticisms. Policy researchers following this model typically are affiliated more often with universities than with independent research institutes or consulting firms. Since the funder is not likely to be the user of the information, researchers following this model must seek out their own audiences for their recommendations. As a result, the researchers run the risk that users will not be found, leading to a study without impact.

In contrast to research funded by "nonusers," policy research can also be funded by an organization specifically interested in using the study results. In this situation, since the funder is also a user, the funder is usually included in the research process to a much greater extent than in the former model. Furthermore, while the researcher may not have the unfettered critical freedom allowed in the previous model, the researcher has a built-in audience for study results. Whether the funding source is also a study user, therefore, has important implications throughout the policy research process.

Policy research varies as to whether the focus is on problem definition or solution. Although policy research is a quest for policy-relevant solutions to social problems, not all social problems are defined either precisely or appropriately enough to permit a search for causes and solutions. For those ill-defined problems, the policy research study may need to focus primarily on problem definition rather than on problem resolution. Doing policy research for problem definitional purposes has been described by Weiss (1977) as the "enlightenment function" of social research.

An example of a policy research study for definitional purposes is described by James Coleman (1975) in his famous study on the equality of educational opportunity. Coleman made the observation that a major contribution of his study was to help policymakers define educational inequality. Previously, inequality had been defined solely in terms of the amount of resources that were put into the educational system. Coleman's study helped to shift attention and understanding away from input and toward the unequal effects of the resources on the children. Once this shift had been attained, different (and presumably more accurate) questions about the causes and solutions to educational inequality could then be pursued. Therefore, many policy research studies may actually focus primarily on shaping policymakers' understanding of the social problem, and by doing so, make the causes and alternative solutions clearer.

Policy research varies as to the organizational setting. Policy research may be conducted in a variety of organizational settings. The organizations may be located within the funding source, such as offices structured to conduct planning, evaluation, policy analysis, research, or development. The organization conducting the research may also be external to the funding source, such as nonprofit think tanks, for-profit contract research firms, consultants, and universities. Although it is unclear how organizational setting affects the rate of utilization or impact of policy research findings (see Meltsner, 1976; Siegel & Doty, 1978; and Weiss, 1978 for discussion), the organizational setting has a definite impact on the research process itself. Research conducted "in house" is generally more constrained by the bureacracy's assumptions and views of social problems; external researchers, on the other hand, tend to have more critical freedom. In addition, in-house researchers may have a better understanding than external researchers of the political and organizational constraints involved in implementing alternative recommendations (Weiss, 1978).

Policy research varies as to the academic discipline of the researcher. Policy researchers hail from a variety of disciplines including psychology, sociology, law, political science, anthropology, economics, and public administration. As the approach taken by researchers to the study of social problems depends on their academic training, policy research efforts tend to reflect this training in the assumption and methods used.

For example, economists originally studying the problem of high fertility rates in developing countries tended to focus exclusively on the relationship between fertility and economic development. Therefore, the argument purported, fertility rates would decrease as economic stability increased. By contrast, health care researchers argued that fertility was a function of the facilities available for providing adequate care to the populace. Finally, psychologists and sociologists focused on the environmental as well as intra- and interpersonal factors that motivate individuals to reduce their birth rates. Obviously, as interest in population research has grown, there has been a greater understanding that no one perspective is sufficient. Nevertheless, disciplinary biases exist. In doing policy research, then, researchers should recognize that their disciplinary backgrounds to some extent will dictate the variables considered and the models advanced.

In summary, policy research refers to a varied group of activities. What ties these different variations together, however, is that they are all focused on helping policymakers to solve social problems.

CHARACTERISTICS OF POLICY RESEARCH STUDIES

Although policy research efforts may vary in a number of ways, there are certain characteristics of the policy research process that differentiate it from other types of research efforts. These characteristics are that policy research

—is multidimensional in focus;
—uses an empirico-inductive research orientation;
—incorporates the future as well as the past;
—responds to study users; and
—explicitly incorporates values.

Each of these characteristics is described below.

Policy research is multidimensional. Public policies typically attempt to resolve complex social problems that are composed of a number of dimensions, factors, effects, and causes. For example, in studying the problem of residential mobility (or lack thereof), mobility could be studied as it relates to disparities in race, industrial growth, or urban/rural sprawl. Mobility could also be studied as it is affected by personal preferences, the adequacy of "infrastructures," or financial status. Finally, mobility could be studied as it is affected by attitudes, economic growth, and crime. Although it is not reasonable to expect that all these elements would be studied in a policy research effort, it *is* reasonable to expect that all these elements would be identified and considered for their effects on the specific elements selected for more focused attention. If solutions to complex social problems are forthcoming, policy research must attempt to study the entire multidimensional nature of the problem.

Policy research uses an empirico-inductive approach. Policy research begins with the social problem and attempts empirically to induce concepts and causal theories as the study of the social problem progresses. Referred to as empirico-inductive, this approach contrasts sharply with the traditional scientific hypothesis-testing approach. The hypothesis-testing approach, in which social phenomena are studied primarily in order to test specific theories, has little place in policy research. While such an approach fosters thoroughness in scientific exploration, the potential loss and misperception of information engendered by taking a singular perspective on a multidimensional problem is too great a risk and luxury for policy researchers. Therefore, a policy researcher does not approach a social problem with a predetermined theory of its causes and effects. Instead, the researcher engages in an iterative process whereby information and model building are constantly interchanged. This type of research approach has been termed by some as the "grounded theory" approach to research (Glaser & Strauss, 1967).

Policy research focuses on malleable variables. In order for policy research to yield action-oriented, implementable recommendations, the research must focus on those aspects of the social problem open to influence and intervention (i.e., malleable variables). For example, research on residential mobility has tended to focus primarily on the immediate precipitants or reasons why families decide to move. As Rossi and Shlay (1982) point out, however, such research has been of little use to policymakers since immediate precipitants tend to be personal (e.g., personal preference), and virtually closed to policy-level influence. Instead, Rossi and Shlay recommend shifting research attention to more malleable variables, such as a description of the structures of residential locations that attract families once they have decided to move. A study that focuses on such malleable variables has a much greater likelihood of producing useful, implementable recommendations.

Policy research is responsive to study users. A critical characteristic of policy research is the identification of study users as one of the first steps in the policy research process. These users may be numerous, varying in expectations, agendas, values, assumptions, and needs. Recognizing that these needs and perceptions may present conflicting demands, the policy researchers must still try to respond to them as much as possible. Meeting some demands is obviously an easier proposition than meeting other demands. For example, if several congressional subcommittees are in the process of developing legislation that could benefit from the ongoing work of a policy researcher, providing interim reports of preliminary recommendations can usually be used to meet such demands. Other demands, however, are not so easily resolved, as when one study user (the funding source) wants to use the study results in a power play and not share them with other users. Although there are no easy answers, suggestions for coping with such situations are offered in Chapter 2.

Policy research explicitly incorporates values. Policy research is a value-laden process, in which many of the decisions involved in the research effort are driven by numerous and sometimes conflicting values. The values of the study users will enter into the processes of defining the social problem, formulating research questions, developing recommendations from the findings, and disseminating the results to the selected audiences. For example, in studying issues affecting the elderly, values enter into such fundamental questions as: How self-reliant should the elderly be? Is it a public or private, family or individual responsibility to care for the elderly? How much socially supported care of the elderly is minimally acceptable? (See Tropman & McClure, 1980, for a discussion of the role of these value positions in social policy research.)

In addition to these values, the normative values of the society-at-large are considered both in designing the research study and in recommending specific courses of action for alleviating the social problem. Finally, the researcher's values will affect the entire research process, from the general study approach selected to the conclusions and recommendations made. Thus, from the outset of the policy research process, the various values and the ways in which the process is altered by these values must be clearly understood.

As indicated by this list of characteristics, policy research is a challenging endeavor. The researcher must be able to consider all aspects of the multidimensional social problem, identify and maintain a focus on the most malleable variables, study the social problem without imposing a predefined theory, consider the effects of both past and future trends on the present, explicitly incorporate values into the research process, and be responsive to study users despite their numerous and sometimes conflicting demands. For these reasons, policy research is rarely done now the way it should be. Research studies tend to consider only a small set of variables, focus exclusively on the present rather than past or future trends, and fail to consider explicitly the role of values. Furthermore, because successful policy research necessitates not only an experienced policy researcher, but an open and attentive policymaker and policymaking environment, truly effective policy research is difficult to achieve.

THE POLICY RESEARCH PROCESS

The policy research process consists of five major activities:

(1) Preparation (Chapter 2)
(2) Conceptualization (Chapter 3)
(3) Technical analysis (Chapter 4)
(4) Recommendations analysis (Chapter 5)
(5) Communication (Chapter 6)

For the policy research study to be successful, all five steps are essential. Preparatory information about the social problem and sociopolitical environment must be gathered; the social problem and research questions must be conceptualized; the analytic approach must be designed and implemented; the recommendations must be analyzed for their feasibility and modified, if necessary; and the study results must be appropriately communicated. Without any one of these activities, the policy researcher runs the risk of producing unused results.

Although each of the five steps are essential to policy research, the extent to which each step is carried out will vary depending on the constraints imposed on the study. The preparation may be done in conjunction with the conceptualization, whereas the recommendations analysis may consist of only a few phone calls and discussions. Furthermore, depending on the policy researcher's professional role, certain steps and activities may be more relevant than others. For example, a consultant may be more likely to focus on the first, second, and fourth steps (preparation, conceptualization, and recommendations), whereas a social scientist contracted primarily to do data collection will more likely be focused on the third step (technical analysis). Despite these possible variations, the researcher needs to clearly understand which activities should be undertaken to constitute a full-scale policy research effort. Then, in streamlining the study, the researcher can more fully appreciate the trade-offs of conducting less extensive efforts. With these thoughts in mind, let us turn to the process by which *you* may contribute to the alleviation of a social problem.

EXERCISES

1. Suppose you, as a policy researcher, are concerned with the social problem of loneliness—that is, the fact that many people go through their lives being lonely. How might you approach this social problem if you were a traditional basic researcher at a university? What would you do first, second, and so on? What would you do with your results? (Hint: As a basic researcher, you start with a theory. . . .) How might you approach the problem of loneliness if you were a policy researcher? In what ways does this approach differ from the basic research approach you just described?

2. Suppose you are a member of a university policymaking committee deciding whether or not to build a new dorm for the students. What might the policy context be for this decision? That is, what types of information might you want the committee to have to make its decision, who do you feel should be involved in the decisionmaking, and what might the various people involved have to gain or lose from the decision?

3. As a policy researcher you decide to study the communist threat in Third World countries. What issues might you focus on if you were a political scientist? What issues might you focus on if you were a psychologist? Compare and contrast these two approaches.

2

Preparing for
a Policy Research Study

Activities involved in the preparation of the study are discussed, including the types of preparatory information to be collected, a methodology for the collection, and issues involved in the decision to conduct policy research.

The policy research process involves much more than designing and implementing a technically appropriate methodological plan or analyzing data. Some of the most important activities in the research process occur *prior to* designing the technical methodology or analysis. These activities focus on the preparation and conceptualization of the policy research study.

Preparatory activities consist primarily of gathering information on such issues as the current and past policymaking context of the selected social problem, the types of study recommendations that would be feasible given the existing sociopolitical environment and the resources needed to conduct a useful study on the social problem. It is also during these preparatory activities that the researcher gathers enough information to decide if a policy research study should be undertaken at this point.

Once preliminary knowledge about the social problem has been acquired and a decision to do the policy research study has been made, activities to conceptualize the study are undertaken. In conceptualizing the study, the preparatory information is used to develop a preliminary model of the social problem, formulate specific research questions, and select appropriate research investigators.

The emphasis in this text on preparatory and conceptualization activities is indicative of the need for policy researchers to position their studies according to existing societal and political conditions. The preparatory activities provide information on these conditions, while the conceptualization activities use that information to position the study. Therefore, the preliminary activities of preparation and conceptualization comprise two very important steps of the policy research process. In this chapter, activities involved in the preparation of the study are discussed. Included in this discussion are the types of preparatory information to be collected, a methodology for collecting the information, and the issues involved in the decision to carry out the policy research effort. Chapter 3 will describe the ways in which the preparatory information is to be used to conceptualize the research effort.

FOCUS OF INFORMATION INQUIRY

To prepare for a policy research study means that the researcher needs to acquire sufficient knowledge to determine the direction which the policy research process should follow if useful recommendations are to result. As research depends to such a large extent on the existing environment, achieving an understanding of that environment is essential if the study is to be successful. Specifically, there are four issues concerning this environment that the researcher should understand before proceeding with the policy research effort. The four issues are as follows:

- the policymaking context of the social problem,
- the range of definitions of and values held about the social problem,
- the types of recommendations about the problem that will be feasible, and
- the resources needed and available to do the study.

It is only after the researcher has achieved a rudimentary understanding of these issues that the decision can be made as to whether a policy research study on the social problem is appropriate at this time.

Policymaking context of the social problem. There are four aspects of the policymaking context to be understood. First, major policy issues related to the social problem—past, present, and projected for the future—need to be identified. For example, the social problem of adequate care for the elderly involves several policy issues. Some of these issues include appropriate health care financing, quality of nursing homes, adequate social security benefits, supportive housing arrangements (e.g., tax incentives for renting homes to family members), fewer incidents of age discrimination, establishment of an acceptable age, developing social programs to care for the elderly homeless, and means to ensure appropriate treatment of the elderly handicapped. By identifying these policy issues, the researcher can begin to understand the multiple dimensions of the selected social problem, as well as the specific aspects of the social problem that have been attended to in the past by the policymakers. As Lewis Dexter (1970, p. 260) found in a study of the legislative process "the most important part of the legislative decision process was the decision about which decision [i.e., issue] to consider."

A second aspect of the policymaking context needing to be understood is the process whereby policy decisions are made about the identified policy issues. The policymaking process involves such elements as the communication channels through which information on the policy issues flow (e.g., vertical or horizontal), the critical gates and decision points through which issues must pass (e.g., the House Ways and Means Committee), and the policy mechanisms typically used in conjunction with the policy issues.

Policy mechanisms refer to tools or vehicles used by policymakers to achieve their policy objectives. There are a vast array of such tools. For example, Table 2.1 presents a list developed by one policy researcher (Joseph Coates, assistant to the director of the congressional Office of Technology Assessment). As shown in the table, tools can be divided into six types. The first type involves mechanisms concerned with dissemination. Using this type implies that a social problem can be alleviated simply by exchanging information about the problem. The second type involves financial incentives and disincentives (e.g., taxes, grants). A mechanism of this type would be used if money was felt to provide the motivating force for alleviating the social problem.

A third type of mechanism includes regulatory and control measures. These mechanisms attempt to alleviate social problems by constraining the range of activities in which an individual or organization can engage. For example, the regulations of the U.S. Environmental Protection Agency which specify the minimum standards for safe, potable water (Safe Drinking Water Act of 1977) constitutes a regulatory mechanism.

A fourth type of mechanism concerns the operation of a policy action. This mechanism is used when action is felt to be a constructive way for alleviating social problems. For example, rather than, or in addition to, regulating minimal standards of clean water, policy researchers can recommend that facilities for treating sewage be built so that clean water can be achieved.

A fifth type of mechanism has been referred to as "symbolic priority-setting" (Nieman & Lovell, 1981) or "policy-related" in Table 2.1. Priority-setting mechanisms involve recommendations which simply indicate that the problem is an important one and worth further attention. While priority-setting mechanisms may be used to delay a decision or make a "nondecision", such a mechanism can occasionally have a dramatic impact on the problem. For example, the discussion in Congress on whether to establish an "industrial policy" for American industrial revitalization is a highly political one. If a decision is reached that makes establishing an industrial policy a priority item in a subsequent Congress, two messages will be communicated to the general public. These two messages are as follows: (a) American industry needs revitalization, and (b) the best way to revitalize industry is to set a national policy that addresses businesses across and within their industrial markets. These two messages would be extremely important for the consumers and businesses of the U.S. economy.

A final type of mechanism not separated out in the table is research and development (R&D). As with priority-setting, R&D can be a "delay tactic." However, occasionally, recommending R&D may establish priorities and

TABLE 2.1
Policy Mechanism*

I. *Information Related*
    Generation of information by means of
        data collection (e.g., census surveys)
        demonstration
        evaluations
        technology assessment
        public (e.g., congressional) hearings
        monitoring
        research and development on
            (a) social cost
            (b) public policy alternatives
            (c) the system
            (d) technology
            (e) basic science
            (f) intervention experiments
    The packaging of information
        as curriculum
        display of pros and cons
    The dissemination of information in terms of
        reports
        seminars
        extension programs
        trade fairs
        conferences, symposia
        state technical services
    Stimulation of interest
        providing a forum
        education
        publicity
        propaganda
        fear and threats
    Withhold information
    Proposing model legislation

II. *Financial Measures*
    Taxes
        Value added tax
        Excise or income tax
        Corporate or personal tax
        Tax write-offs or subsidies
        Depreciation and Depletion Allowances
    Grants
    Contracts
    Loans
    Rewards for innovation and invention
    Incentives (e.g., matching funds, scholarships, loans, grants)
    Earmarking funds, setting floors and ceilings
    Insure loans, crops, investments, etc.
    Compensate for loss

Table 2.1 (Continued)

Underwrite
Set priorities on funding
Allocate funds

III. *Regulatory and Control Measures*
Regulate/deregulate
Legislate
Set standards
Certify
License
Codes
Government control or monopoly
Codes
Grant rights
Form interstate compacts
Court decisions, injunctions
Cease and desist orders
Monopoly privileges
Inspection requirements
Fines and punitive damages
Registration and mandatory reporting
Audit
Substitute criminal for civil sanctions or vice versa
Institutionalize
Rationing
Quotas
Limit liability
Import
Export
Copyrights
Patents
Prohibitions
Ban
Require warranties
Zone
Eminent domain
Declare martial law

IV. *Operation*
Building civil works
Build facilities (e.g., drug treatment centers)
Operate facilities (e.g., traffic control systems)
Establishment or support of an industrial base by government purchase
Demonstrate

V. *Policy Related Function*
Setting of policy
Defining priorities
Set objectives
Delayed decisions
Coordinate affairs

*Adapted from Coates (1978).

directions in a more acceptable manner than other mechanisms. For example, Congress was willing to accept appropriation of R&D funds for studying ways to house intercontinental ballistic missiles (ICBMs). However, Congress was not willing to endorse ICBMs or their basing to the general public. By appropriating R&D funds, movement toward a strong defense system could continue without congressional members appearing hawkish to their supporters back home.

Given the range of policy mechanisms available to policymakers (see Lowi, 1964; Salisbury & Heinz, 1968; or Wade, 1972, for further discussions of policy mechanisms), it is important to understand which mechanisms are appropriate for which policy issues. For example, the policy issue concerning the public use of seatbelts illustrates the selective appropriateness of certain policy mechanisms. Regulations that either mandate automatically closing seatbelts or make it a crime to drive beltless are mechanisms that are only beginning to receive support. Instead, policy mechanisms that have received greater public backing in the past include the practice of providing financial incentives for "buckling up" to drivers and companies with high employee accident rates, and the use of passive restraints (APA Monitor, 1982). Suggestions for selecting acceptable policy mechanisms such as these are discussed in more detail in Chapter 3 (see the section entitled "Identify Malleable Variables").

A third aspect of the policymaking context that needs to be considered is the set of key actors or *"stakeholders."* Stakeholders are those individuals or groups of individuals who either have some input into the decisionmaking process or are affected by policy decisions on the social problem. By identifying stakeholders, the actual and potential users of the policy research study can be delineated, allowing the research effort to be molded to their needs. Stakeholders may include any number of different people or organizations. For example, stakeholders can include congressional leaders, staffers, committees, and subcommittees; government agencies; personnel at federal, regional, and state levels of government; general constituency groups (e.g., Common Cause); special interest groups; and local or community leaders. As an illustration, there were numerous stakeholders involved in a policy research study for Congress on the ability of states to assess the effectiveness of their social service block grant programs. The stakeholders included the funder (Assistant Secretary for Planning and Evaluation, DHHS); the agency responsible for the study (Office of Human Development Services, DHHS); the congressional committees that requested the report (Senate Finance Committee and House Ways and Means Committee); state government offices, such as the State Social Service Agencies and evaluation departments; and special interest groups, such as American Public Welfare Association, United Way, and the National Governors Association (Majchrzak, Schroeder, & Patchen, 1982).

The final aspect of the policymaking context which needs to be understood is the power structure of the policymaking process. As stakeholders are identified, it is important to differentiate between those who are key decisionmakers, those who are influential, and those with little existing power who are victims of others' decisions on these issues. For example, if congressional action encouraging the use of advanced technology in manufacturing industries were studied, the powerful decisionmakers might be members of the congressional Joint Economic Committee; influential organizations might include the National Association of Manufacturers and the AFL-CIO; and the affected constituents with little power might be the displaced workers. By identifying the differential power of the stakeholders, a more realistic picture of which group will act on the research recommendations and which group will be affected by those recommendations is achieved.

In sum, an understanding of the policymaking context involves knowing the major policy issues, knowing the process by which decisions on the policy issues are reached, identifying stakeholders in the policymaking process, and delineating the power structure involved in the policy decisionmaking. Suggestions for carrying out these activities are described later in this chapter.

Definitions of and values held about social problems. In addition to context, the sociopolitical environment involves the range of definitions, assumptions, and values that stakeholders hold about the social problem. By acquiring an understanding of these opinions, the researchers can make preliminary judgments about how difficult it will be to do policy research on the selected social problem. That is, if there is little agreement on what the problem is, and these definitions are riddled with inflexible values and assumptions, conducting a policy research study that will make a significant contribution alleviating the social problem may be difficult, at best. For example, in doing his study on educational inequality, Coleman (1975) recognized that educational equality had not been defined adequately for it to be achieved. Therefore, his study needed to focus on fleshing out the different values and assumptions underlying educational equality and thereby attempt some resolution.

In acquiring information on definitions and values, the researcher should first identify the theories that the different stakeholders have about the social problem, its causes, and its potential solutions. The way a stakeholder defines a social problem is essentially "an opinion of whether the phenomenon is or is not a problem" (Lindblom & Cohen, 1979, p. 49). That is, the problem definition is a statement by the stakeholder of what needs are felt to be important, and what threshold of need fulfillment is not currently being met. For example, one stakeholder may define the unemployment problem as the failure to meet individuals' needs for earned wages (an individual level of analysis). In contrast, another stakeholder may define the unemployment problem in purely economic terms (i.e., as the failure of the U.S. economy to meet minimal employment standards for national productivity growth).

The way in which a problem is defined (and the solutions sought) will determine to a large extent the stakeholders' beliefs about causes and potential solutions to the problem. For example, unemployment defined in terms of individuals' needs will result in a search for causes and solutions involving individual workers (e.g., job retraining programs). In contrast, unemployment defined in national productivity terms will yield a focus on options for improving growth in high unemployment industries. Obviously, these different definitions will lead to different approaches to alleviating the social problem.

After stakeholders' models of the social problem have been identified, values and assumptions about the models need to be clarified. Such values include the level of responsibility and sacrifice that society should accept in striving to alleviate the social problem. For example, should the public welfare structure be geared toward providing support at home for impoverished mothers of young children or should it be designed to enable these mothers to work by providing day care? (Maccoby et al., 1983). Should government programs be designed to catch welfare cheats, even if such programs deny or delay welfare for the honest majority? (Wildavsky, 1979). If the full range of relevant opinions are to be known, answers to these very personal and revealing value questions must be elicited by the policy researcher. Finally, in acquiring information on stakeholders' assumptions and definitions, it is essential to understand the flexibility (vulnerability) of these opinions. The more flexible the opinion, the greater the likelihood that the policy research effort will be able to promote change.

Types of feasible recommendations. A third issue with which the policy researcher should be familiar concerns the types of recommendations that would be feasible given the particular sociopolitical environment. The question that must be answered is this: What types of recommendations advocating what general types of changes are acceptable and implementable? Once this question can be answered, the policy researcher is in a much better position to determine if the proposed research is worth pursuing.

Addressing the issue of recommendations necessitates an understanding of two subissues: (1) the degree of change that can be tolerated by the cultural and political environment, and (2) the potential uses of the policy research study by that environment.

The degree of tolerable change can be described by the continuum presented below.

```
|_____|_____|
Incremental            Mixed Scanning            Fundamental
```

Incremental change is change that focuses on fairly minor, short-term solutions within the framework of existing major goals and assumptions. In contrast, fundamental change tends to be more far-reaching, offering new perspectives, assumptions, and goals. Between the two extremes is a type of change referred to as "mixed scanning" (Etzioni, 1976). Change of the mixed scanning variety involves the formulation of fundamentally new guidelines that are to be modified incrementally over time. In attempting to identify types of feasible recommendations, then, the policy researcher must determine the degree of change the sociopolitical environment will accept.

A situation in which an acceptable degree of change was important was described in a 1976 issue of the *National Journal Reports* (as cited in Wildavsky, 1979). In this issue, then President Carter was described as expressing an overwhelming preference for fundamental rather than incremental changes. Carter is quoted as follows:

> Most of the controversial issues that are not routinely well-addressed can only respond to a comprehensive approach. Incremental efforts to make basic changes are often foredoomed to failure because the special interest groups can benefit from the status quo and focus their attention on increments that most affect themselves, and the general public can't be made either interested or aware. (July 17, 1976, p. 999)

Thus policy research studies directed at President Carter would probably have needed to focus more on fundamental than on incremental changes if the recommendations were to be heard.

In addition to determining the degree of tolerable change, the policy researcher also needs to assess the potential uses of the policy research study. A policy research study might be used to assist in the formulation of the problem or its solution. Policy research may also be used to evaluate alternative policy options. Finally, policy research may be used for less desirable purposes, such as to excuse a lack of definitive action or to provide decisionmakers with political ammunition for their constituents. Despite the less altruistic nature of these latter uses, such uses do not preclude the possibility that the study will make an intellectual contribution as well (see Rein & White, 1977, for examples).

Needed and available resources to do study. A final issue regarding the environment to be understood is the minimum type and level of general resources needed (and available) to conduct the desired policy research effort. Resources include not only financial needs, but also amount and expertise of facilities, personnel, and equipment. For example, a study on military recruiting requirements in the year 2000 might necessitate not only a certain funding level,. but also the access to and the ability to comprehend confidential documents on personnel requirements of new weapons systems.

While obtaining information on resources, policy researchers must remember to ascertain the *minimum* level of needed resources and recognize study limitations that these minimal levels will impose. Occasionally, large policy research studies have been done, such as the Westinghouse Head Start evaluation described by Cicirelli et al. (1969), and the New Jersey Income Maintenance experiment described by Watts (1971). However, reductions in funding, the need to respond quickly to decisionmakers, and a greater realization of the dynamic nature of social problems suggest that smaller, quick studies are becoming the rule (Schmidt, 1982). This model of doing small, quick studies is particularly suitable for government in-house research efforts since such efforts must frequently address questions and inquiries posed by media attention (Ginsburg, 1982). In addition, however, such small studies can also be done in more academic settings, such as one done by Caputo and Cole (1975). In this study, the research effort was small enough to have been supported entirely by a little time from the authors, their graduate assistants, and from data processing. Despite the low level of effort, their study was still able to draw some interesting policy conclusions. In sum, the model of a small and quick, rather than large and long policy research effort may be the preferred future mode for policy research.

STEPS TO INFORMATION INQUIRY

As described in the previous section, preparatory activities involve acquiring an understanding of four issues: (1) policymaking context of the social problem, (2) range of opinions about the social problem, (3) types of feasible recommendations, and (4) needed and available resources. To acquire this understanding, the policy researcher must obtain information from several different sources. In this section, an eight-step approach to gathering and synthesizing this information is suggested. This approach is offered as only one of many possible methods that can be used in the preparation of policy research. You are encouraged to modify this approach as the demands of your policy research efforts change.

Below are listed the eight steps to acquiring an understanding of the sociopolitical environment.

Step 1. Select social problem
Step 2. Identify key policy issues
Step 3. Analyze legislative history of policy issues
Step 4. Trace progress of previous research and change efforts
Step 5. Obtain organizational charts of decisionmaking bodies
Step 6. Draw model of policymaking process
Step 7. Interview stakeholders
Step 8. Synthesize information

Step 1: Select social problem. To prepare for a policy research effort, the researcher begins with some vague notion of the social problem. For example, in an early analysis of the utility of social science research, Robert Lynd (1939) presented a list of social problems about which social science should be concerned. For Lynd, such problems included the planning and control of urbanization, prevention of war, quality of life for the masses, and the maintenance of democratic principles in modern life.

The precise social problem selected will depend to some extent on the circumstances in which the research effort was initiated. A study may be specifically commissioned by a client who is interested in a specific social problem. In this case, agreeing to work for the client is tantamount to selecting the social problem of interest to the client. For example, if the U.S. Department of Labor (DOL) is interested in developing policy options for reemploying displaced workers, DOL may disseminate a request for proposal (RFP) to policy researchers familiar with the social problem. The RFP will typically contain a statement of the problem, a general outline of how the research study might proceed, and the resource limits for the study. In response to the RFP, a policy researcher may decide to submit a proposal which details a specific approach to the problem and the expertise that he or she would bring to the study. The client (DOL in this case) will then select the most qualified researcher and the study will begin.[1]

In contrast to policy researchers doing studies in which the social problem is selected by the client, policy researchers may also select their own social problems. For example, Robert Lynd may have been interested in the social problems brought about by urbanization. Given his interest, he might have approached a government agency (e.g., U.S. Department of Housing and Urban Development), a foundation (e.g., Rockefeller Foundation), or have used university resources to pursue options for alleviating the problems. Without support for his pursuit, research on the problems of interest would have had to be postponed. For policy researchers in academic settings, it is the rare situation that no support is obtainable to study a social problem of concern.

Step 2: Identify key policy issues. Having selected a social problem, the key policy issues must be identified. Typically, the key policy issues relevant to that problem will become apparent as the problem is selected and more completely understood. For example, prevention of war involves, at a minimum, policies concerning foreign strategic weapons, foreign trade, weapons research and development, and economic conditions at home and abroad.

While the key issues will generally be obvious, there are occasions when they are not immediately apparent. In such situations, consult information sources such as subject matter experts, classic writings on the social problem, newspapers, and groups which may be interested in the problem. For example, the NAACP might be contacted if the problem you pick is racial discrimination and you are unaware of the key policy issues. In the process of identifying key issues, you may discover that there are too many issues to be adequately incorporated into one study. In such a situation, more narrowly defining the problem to focus on only one or two issues may be appropriate.

Step 3: Analyze legislative history of policy issues. In this third step, the historical natures of the issues are traced from their inauguration as subjects of policy attention to their current legislative status at all appropriate levels of government. The quickest way to trace legislative history is to obtain the most recently passed legislation on the issues. This legislation usually references earlier statutes and sometimes even explains why it was necessary to supplement earlier legislation with more recent action. In addition to acquiring the actual legislation, the researcher may find other sources helpful for a historical analysis of the issues. These other sources will be particularly important if the social problem has received little legislative attention in the past. Such sources may include previous political analyses of the policy issues by political scientists, writings by politically active individuals interested in the issues (e.g., Daniel Patrick Moynihan on urban policy), and statements by experts with historical perspective on the issue.

To analyze the legislative history, researchers should scrutinize their sources for the following information:

(1) Manifest and latent purposes of the legislation (Are the manifest and latent goals similar? Have they changed over time? Are the goals only symbolic or are they intended to create real change?)

(2) Definitions of the social problem to which the legislation is addressed (Have these definitions changed over time or among different supporters?)

(3) Values and assumptions inherent in the legislation
(4) Success and problems of previous legislation
(5) Constituencies affected by legislation (What is the public interest in this policy issue? Who gets hurt or helped by it?)
(6) Key decisionmakers and decisionmaking process (What congressional committees and executive departments were/are involved in the legislation?)
(7) Policy mechanisms used in previous legislation (By what means is the legislation enforced and/or implemented?)

Since this analysis is being done very early in the policy research process, complete detail on each of these seven points is not expected. Rather, a general understanding of these issues should be acquired before proceeding to the next step.

Step 4: Trace process of research or change efforts. For most policy issues, more than one previous or current research effort has been undertaken. Such additional efforts should be identified, and their paths from inception to use of findings should be traced. These efforts can be identified through many of the same sources used in the third step. In tracing previous and current research or change efforts, the researcher should look for the following information:

(1) organizations (i.e., stakeholders and researchers) involved in the research or change efforts,
(2) past uses of research for decisionmaking on this issue,
(3) key decisionmakers and users of research, and
(4) current existence of similar research efforts.

This information will provide insights into the potential use of your research effort, as well as the process by which your study would be used. To obtain this information, you may want to consult directly with researchers involved in studies similar to the one you may be considering. Insights from discussions with other researchers may prove particularly helpful for conceptualizing your study.

Step 5: Obtain organizational charts of decisionmaking bodies. Based on information obtained in the third and fourth steps, you should be able to identify the major decisionmaking bodies involved in the selected policy issues (e.g., Department of Health and Human Services, Department of Defense, Office of Management and Budget, congressional committees). In this fifth step, charts describing generally the organization of these bodies should be obtained or constructed. These charts will indicate positions of authority, describe the communication flow, and delineate major gatekeepers in the decisionmaking process within each organization. This information will promote a better understanding of the decisionmaking process involved in your selected policy issues.

Step 6: Draw model of policymaking process. In steps three through five, preliminary information on various aspects of the policymaking context were obtained. This information included identifying communication channels through which information on the policy issues flows, the critical decision points through which policy decisions must pass, problems which future policies must overcome, stakeholders in the policymaking process, and the power structure of the stakeholders. In this sixth step, the obtained information is synthesized into a preliminary illustration of the policymaking process. Figure 2.1 presents a simple hypothetical example of such a model. As illustrated in this model, policymakers on any one issue may range from local agencies to social service administrators to the state governor and legislature.

Step 7: Interview stakeholders. After drawing a model of the policymaking process, the stakeholders identified in the model should be interviewed. Since a model of the policymaking process for a typical policy issue contains numerous stakeholders, it may not be possible to interview them all. Therefore, the stakeholders will need to be ranked subjectively in order of their relative power and interest in the policy issue. For example, the budget office of a certain state social service agency (as portrayed in Figure 2.1) may serve primarily an accounting function for that agency. Given the relative neutrality of such a position, the budget director probably will not need to be interviewed. A different stakeholder with stronger opinions and more influence, however, may need to be interviewed. In Figure 2.1, the Citizens' Oversight Committee, which serves as a public advocacy representative in many states, would constitute such a stakeholder.

The interviews of the stakeholders can be done formally or informally, either in person or by phone. During these interviews, the following information should be obtained:

- Modifications to the preliminary model of the policymaking process drawn in Step 6 (including the identification of additional stakeholders)
- Definitions, values, and assumptions held by stakeholders about the social problem
- Openness of stakeholders to new directions for alleviating the social problem
- Ways in which stakeholders expect to use a policy research study on the social problem
- Acceptability and implementability of different types of recommendations

In order to obtain this information, interviews may need to vary with the specific personality of each stakeholder. As the policy issues being dis-

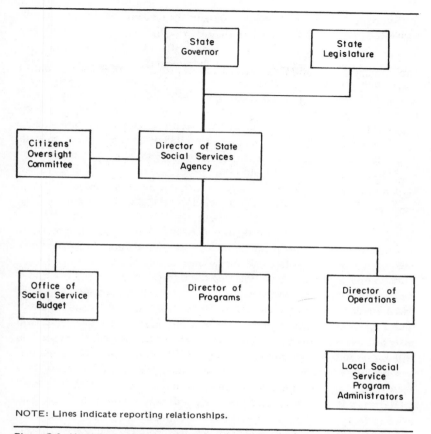

NOTE: Lines indicate reporting relationships.

Figure 2.1 Hypothetical Model of a Policymaking Process for a State Social Service Agency

cussed are typically controversial, stakeholders will generally be wary of the way information they provide may be used. They will be concerned about the political preferences of the policy researcher and whether their views will be represented fairly. Therefore, in doing interviews, it may be necessary to use different approaches to encourage stakeholders to talk. Some stakeholders may be more comfortable sharing information through anecdotal stories told over cocktails; other stakeholders may prefer interviews to be formal and taped with transcripts reviewed for accuracy. Since the purposes of these interviews are to obtain preliminary information and establish a contact for gathering further information later on, any approach that puts the stakeholder at ease should be used.

To conduct the interviews, several suggestions may be helpful. First, many stakeholders may not know their own values and assumptions. For example, an employer interviewed about racially discriminatory hiring and promotion practices may not consciously realize that the practices reflect this own racial biases. Nor might a stakeholder who values higher education for the poor realize the consequences and trade-offs that such a value may entail. Finally, stakeholders may not want to discuss their values since they may be afraid that the values will be misinterpreted and used against them.

In such situations, values may be best elicited by observing or discussing past behaviors (e.g., actions) on earlier stated policies (e.g., earlier speeches made by the stakeholder). In addition, "people are most useful in revealing values in response to specific analyses, concepts, and proposals" (Coates, 1978, p. 68). The aids most useful for eliciting stakeholders' personal opinions about a social problem include presenting them with hypothetical scenarios or conceptual models of the social problem, listing alternative needs and values that the social problem might concern, and presenting different perspectives of the problem and having them react to each.

A second suggestion for conducting the interviews is to recognize that it may be to the political advantage of some stakeholders not to state their values and definitions explicitly (Wildavsky, 1979). By refusing to commit to a particular perspective, they may be able to avoid alienating constituents. You must be careful not to cajole such stakeholders into a position. However, you will also need to recognize that a sociopolitical environment comprised primarily of them may make a useful research study difficult to achieve.

A third suggestion for conducting the interviews is to use "if . . . then" scenarios to determine both the openness of the environment to change, and the feasibility of different types of recommendations. By presenting such scenarios, stakeholders can react to a specific concept or action by indicating their willingness and ability to support such a change.

Finally, during the course of the interviews, the researcher should try to assess whether the stakeholder is sufficiently committed to the study to provide advice, feedback, and/or additional resources during the course of the study. For example, if the interview ends with a solicitation for help or a commitment to answer questions in the future, the stakeholder may be flattered and opportunistic enough to provide advice as the study progresses. From the policy researcher's standpoint, such input later in the process may prove particularly valuable in interpreting research results and developing implementable recommendations. (And who knows? Maybe the stakeholder will be so enamored of the researcher that she or he will provide additional resources so that a more comprehensive study of the social problem can be undertaken!)

Step 8: Synthesize information. In this final step of the preparatory activities, the information that has been obtained in the previous seven steps is synthesized. This synthesis addresses the following series of questions:

(1) Who are the study users? Of those users, who are decisionmakers with the most to gain from the study? Do they have sufficient decisionmaking power and commitment, as well as appropriate expectations about the study to enable its completion and successful utilization?
(2) How open is the sociopolitical environment to change and to what extent?
(3) What resources are necessary to conduct a study which provides meaningful results to its users? Are available resources sufficient?

To answer the first series of questions involves a close look at the model constructed of the policymaking process, notes of the interviews with the stakeholders, and information on the legislative history of the selected policy issues. In synthesizing this information, you should also try to identify and promote a "champion" of the study. A champion is a powerful decisionmaker willing to support your research. Jo Fraatz (1982) suggests that congressional representatives likely to be champions include those with long-term reputations as specialists in the social problem, those with a histories of relationships to researchers, and those who are newcomers anxious to establish reputations. Senators Edward Kennedy, Walter Mondale, and Daniel Inouye, for example, have been past champions of policy research. If the researcher can seek out such champions, the likelihood of producing a useful study is greatly enhanced.

The second set of questions, regarding openness to change involves the synthesis of information on values, assumptions, and definitions. For an environment to be open to change, there must be a fair amount of consensus (or potential consensus) on the social problem, opinions must currently or potentially be fairly flexible, and support for recommendations must be accessible. In synthesizing the information to address these issues, Frank Fischer (1980) recommends a technique called "value mapping." In value mapping, the norms and values of a particular problem are sorted out, either quantitatively (e.g., by assigning importance weights to certain dimensions of the problem), or qualitatively (e.g., by constructing a model of the network of values surrounding the problem). Whether use of such a formal procedure as value mapping is indicated should depend on the complexity of the problem and on the available time. For less complex problems and/or research that must be done quickly, a more informal synthesis of the information may be sufficient.

The final series of questions, about study resources, needs also to be addressed in this synthesis. For example, decisions need to be made about whether the social problem is best addressed by a small consulting effort or a full-scale research project. The amount of time before a major policy decision must be reached on the issue should be determined. Finally, other decision points for which a policy research study could provide input should be identified. Addressing these considerations is essential before further work on the social problem is undertaken.

DECISION TO CONDUCT THE STUDY

The final preparatory activity involves the decision as to whether the policy research study should be conducted. Since there may be numerous situations in which a policy research study should *not* be conducted, this decision must be considered carefully. Before the decision can be made, however, answers to the two following questions must be obtained:

(1) Given the study users, sociopolitical environment, and resources, is a useful policy research study feasible?
(2) If such a study is feasible, am I the right person to do it?

The first question involves reviewing the conclusions reached in synthesizing the preparatory information (Step 8 above). These conclusions will have specified users' needs that must be addressed, discussed the openness of the environment to change, and weighed the amount of resources needed against those available. Thus, these conclusions will indicate the likelihood that a policy research study will help study users in making future policy decisions.

The second question addresses the issue of who should conduct the study. Such factors to be considered include the appropriateness of your technical research skills, the personality match between you and the study users, and the appropriateness of your organizational affiliation for the research. For example a study on the equality of educational opportunities, which is conducted by NAACP researchers, will probably be biased (or be viewed by others as biased) against finding educational equality. If the intent of the study is to influence congressional leaders, such a study is probably best performed by less partial researchers.

Obviously, if you have gone to the trouble of gathering the preparatory information, you probably have every intention of personally conducting the study. However, you owe it to yourself and to the study to assess your skills and personality critically in relation to that which is needed. For example, if efforts to alleviate the social problem at this point clearly necessitate a complicated cost-benefit analysis of two different policy options, the policy researchers should have the skills to do such an analysis. If a study of the social problem that impartially compares the policies preferred by two opposing political parties is needed, the policy researcher needs to be able to provide such an impartial study. If breakthroughs in alleviating the social problem are only possible through some fundamental restructuring of the problem, the policy researcher must be able to have the intellectual capacity for such innovative thinking. If there is not an adequate match between your skills/personality and those needed to do the study, several options are available to you. You may

(1) Supplement your skills with those of additional researchers,
(2) replace yourself as the principal investigator while maintaining a role on the research team, or
(3) turn the study over to someone else.

None of these options may be an easy one; nevertheless, it is better to extricate yourself early from a study that is likely to be poorly done, than wait until later when extrication may no longer be possible.

In sum, the decision to conduct a policy research study must be a subjective one. Only you can decide if a study would be useful and if you are the appropriate one to do it. Given the subjective nature of the decision, you may early in your career find it helpful to establish criteria for determining when you should undertake a policy research effort. The following criteria are those used by the Office of Technology Assessment (OTA) in deciding to study a particular issue (Gibbons, 1983):

• Is the policy issue controversial enough to need objective information?
• Is there enough information on the issue to give objective advice?
• Is the requesting congressional committee the committee that can act on the issue if action is recommended?
• Is OTA the appropriate organization to conduct the study (as opposed to GAO, CBO, or CRS)?[2]

You may want to begin thinking about what your own criteria should be for deciding to conduct a policy research study.

A final word of advice: Once you have decided to conduct a study, clearly identify time frames, procedures for communicating with study users, role expectations (e.g., consultant, change agent, advocate, data collector, or analyst), and the use of information once the study is completed (e.g., confidentiality, release dates). By establishing these rules and procedures prior to beginning the study, unfortunate misunderstandings later on can be avoided.

EXERCISES

1. List all of the questions you need to ask yourself and others when you prepare for a policy research study. Group the questions by the eight steps described in the chapter.

2. The following is a list of social problems. Select one and describe how you would acquire an understanding of the sociopolitical environment to alleviate the social problem. (Follow the eight steps described in this chapter.)

- acid rain
- illegal immigration from Mexico
- increased technological superiority of international automobile manufacturers
- deficits in the social security system
- child abuse

3. Suppose you are a researcher in a consulting firm and are asked by the Office of the Assistant Secretary of Defense (OSD) to conduct a study of the effect of women in the military. You feel that including women in military combat is a commendable step forward for women's rights. However, as you prepare for the study, you discover that the OSD is covertly opposed to women in the military and would like to have evidence to support a policy excluding women from future military service. Do you feel that a fair policy research study yielding useful recommendations could be conducted? If not, what conditions, if any, could you specify to ensure the fairness and utility of the study?

NOTES

1. This description has been grossly simplified. In reality, there will typically be negotiations back and forth and rewriting of proposals before selection and study initiation.

2. GAO is the U.S. General Accounting Office, CBO is the Congressional Budget Office, and CRS is the Congressional Research Service. Like OTA, these three offices conduct forms of research for Congress.

3

Conceptualizing
the Policy Research Study

In this chapter activities involved in the conceptualization of the study are discussed. Included in this discussion are the development of a preliminary model of the social problem, the formulation of specific research questions, and the selection of research investigators.

As part of the preparatory activities described in Chapter 2, you will have decided whether or not a policy research study was appropriate, given the existing sociopolitical environment. Assuming that you have decided to conduct the research study, you will be ready for activities that help you to conceptualize it. Conceptualizing a policy research study involves the three following activities:

(1) developing a preliminary model of the social problem
(2) formulating specific research questions
(3) selecting research investigators

DEVELOP A PRELIMINARY MODEL OF THE SOCIAL PROBLEM

Social scientists doing policy-oriented research have been roundly criticized in the past for lack of clarity and understanding of issues being addressed, simplistic analyses, and narrow, poorly defined foci (Aaron, 1978; Lamm, 1978). To avoid these criticisms, the first step in conceptualizing the research study should be the development of a preliminary model of the social problem. Such a model should generally delineate the definitions, assumptions, values, and presumed causes of the social problem. The developed model is only preliminary as it will be modified when the policy research process progresses.

Figure 3.1 presents two simplified models of a hypothetical social problem discussed by Meehan (1971). In Model A, the nutritional problems of ghetto children are perceived to be a function of parental ignorance that can be altered by parent education programs and improvements in the poor cultural climate of the ghetto. In contrast, Model B proposes that the nutritional deficiencies of ghetto children are a function of the poor economic conditions of ghetto parents. If Model A were used for the study, the types of research questions tested in the study would be very different than if Model

B were used. Therefore, the model of the social problem to be followed must be specified as the first step in conceptualizing the research study prior to formulating the research questions.

To develop a preliminary model of the social problem, the researcher will need to rely primarily on the information gathered as part of the activities described in Chapter 2, as well as on any literature review that the researcher has done to this point. Information gathered from the interviews with the stakeholders will be particularly important. However, when using the stakeholders' comments, researchers should not simply restate their definitions and opinions. To simply accept a stakeholder's problem statement "may be largely surrendering that very objectivity which makes science potentially useful to man in confronting his dilemmas. In so doing, the social scientist may take on the nearsightedness which is such a marked aspect of a culture of 'practical' men floundering in the search for little remedies for large troubles" (Lynd, 1939, pp. 120-121). To illustrate, stakeholders may define racial desegregation as the extent to which "white" (Caucasian) people comply with mandates to decrease racial polarization in urban environments. This definition, however, may represent a narrow or biased view of the problem. An alternative problem definition might include both the voluntary as well as involuntary behavior of black and nonblack ethnic groups toward racial separation (Finsterbusch & Motz, 1980).

In developing a single model of the social problem from the available information, the researcher typically finds that the stakeholders may actually hold conflicting models of the same social problem. For example, a recent survey of 43 state legislators revealed two competing formulations of air pollution: For one set of legislators, pollution was perceived as a question of economics; for the other set, pollution was a health and environmental issue (Maggiotto & Bowman, 1982). Legislators with an economic orientation were more willing to accept environmental deterioration and were opposed to governmental intervention. Legislators with a health/environmental orientation had opposite views; government was perceived to be a primary vehicle in preventing any further deterioration in air quality.

In situations where conflicting views arise, the researcher should first try to build consensus among the stakeholders by developing new models of the social problem that accommodate both opinions. If consensus cannot be achieved in this fashion, one of two options can be pursued. First, attempts to develop a more general model that appeals to "higher-order values" can be undertaken. Higher-order values are those that the general public tends to accept as goals for society at large. Table 3.1 presents examples of such values. By appealing to these higher-order values with which most people agree, the researcher is more likely to obtain agreement on a single model of the social problem.

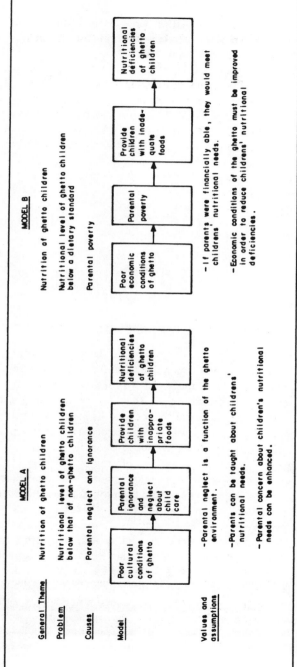

Figure 3.1 Example Models of a Hypothetical Social Problem

45

TABLE 3.1
Examples of Higher-Order Values
for Four Authors

G. Grob (1981)
   abolish poverty
   provide for groups unable to survive independently
   control crime
   improve conditions of work

H. Lasswell (1958)
   well-being
   affection
   skill
   enlightenment

F. Fischer (1980)
   social justice
   public interest

R. Angell (1965)
   dignity
   civil and religious liberties
   peace
   responsible democracy
   humanitarianism

The second option for handling situations lacking consensus on the model of the social problem is to conclude that the conflicting opinions are a function of a lack of information about or attention to the social problem. This conclusion implies that it is only with additional information or attention applied to the social problem that consensus might be reached. With such an option, then, the study itself can be perceived as providing the additional information necessary to build consensus on the social problem.

An example of this second option was offered by Coleman (1975). Because there was such a diversity of opinion about educational equality, the main contribution of Coleman's study on the problem was to build consensus about its definition. According to Coleman (1975), his study provided the information necessary to shift policy attention away from a traditional theory of educational inequality (i.e., inequality defined in terms of amount of resources allocated) to a new theory of inequality. This new theory perceived differences in outcomes as a function of a variety of factors, above and beyond the effects attributable to differences in resource allocations. Although his study did not provide feasible recommendations for alleviating the inequality problem, it clearly provided valuable policy-relevant information.

Finally, there are occasional situations when different models of a social problem have been advanced in such a way that data cannot create consensus. For example, a social problem concerned with the right to have abortions would generate two different models. In the Right to Life model, fetuses are human beings with feelings and emotions, and, therefore, should be allowed to live despite the desires of the mother. In the pro-abortion model, on the other hand, fetuses have not been born yet and, therefore, are not human beings. To decide between the two models would necessitate a consensus on personal values. Data will help little in this regard. In such a situation, then, the policy research effort would need to focus on issues that either explicitly select one model over another, or that do not necessitate the involvement of either model to identify causes and solutions.

In summary, the task of developing a model of the social problem may be neither straightforward nor simple. However, keep in mind that the model you develop at this point is only preliminary. It need not delineate all the causes or variables—only help to point you in the right direction.

FORMULATE SPECIFIC RESEARCH QUESTIONS

After a preliminary model of the social problem is developed, specific research questions can be formulated. Since these questions will drive the methodological plan and eventual implications of the study, their formulation should be undertaken with great care and deliberation. The process of carefully formulating specific research questions involves four sequential steps. First, the researcher must decide what type of impact is desired by the study. Second, a focus (or aspect) of the social problem must be selected. Third, given the variables resulting from the desired impact and focus, the most malleable variables must be identified. Finally, the specific research questions are formulated around the malleable variables most likely to lead to the desired impact on the aspect of the social problem.

Step 1: Decide on the type of impact desired. The first step in formulating research questions is to decide on the type of impact the study should have on the policy environment. Research questions can be directed at several different types of impacts. They can lead to better definitions of the social problem, or if sufficient information already exists, they can identify and/or compare alternative solutions. Research questions can also differ in the extent of impact desired. That is, some research questions search for incremental change, while others focus on more fundamental solutions to the social problem. Finally, research questions can vary in the audience to be affected by the study. Some questions are directed at the highest policymaking level (e.g., President, Congress, or a firm's chief executive officer), while other questions are focused at lower levels (e.g., agency decisionmakers, state or local leaders, or plant managers).

Given the possible variation in the types of impacts that can be achieved by a policy research study, the researcher needs to assess the sociopolitical environment to determine the most feasible type of impact. This assessment should look at the environment's openness to change, the extent to which values and definitions conflict, and the level in the policymaking context at which change could be implemented.

For example, Margaret Boeckmann (1976) suggests that incremental studies are most appropriate for audiences who share the basic values and definitions of the theory of the social problem. In contrast, Jo Fraatz (1982) suggests that social problems with a long history of stormy political debate may need to be addressed by more fundamental research questions. Incremental research questions simply fuel the continuing debate. Finally, in a recent survey of policy research centers (Nagel & Neef, 1978), a popular complaint among center directors was that policy research studies were too often addressed at top-level policymakers who were not involved in developing the actual strategies for implementing the policy. For some social problems, then, the actual success of a policy will be dependent on lower-level staff preparing and implementing regulations, rather than the higher-level policymakers.

Step 2: Select an aspect of the social problem. The second step in formulating research questions is to select an aspect or aspects of the social problem to be studied. Unquestionably, the more multifaceted, multidimensional the research question, the greater the likelihood that the study will produce comprehensive and meaningful results. However, it is unrealistic to expect that a study can encompass all aspects of the problem. Therefore, some guidelines for choosing aspects on which to focus are provided.

Adopting Amitai Etzioni's theory of societal guidance (1976), the researcher can divide a social problem into four focuses. A problem and its causes can be understood first from a *technical* perspective (e.g., the empirical relationship between a 55 mph speed limit and accident rates). Second, a social problem can be understood from the perspective of its *organizational* structure (e.g., mechanisms by which a 55 mph speed limit is implemented) Third, a social problem can be understood in terms of the *societal consensus* (e.g., society's acceptance of the speed limit). Finally, the problem can be understood from a *power* perspective (e.g., the role of auto and oil industries in maintaining the speed limit at 55 mph).

In selecting an aspect of the social problem on which to focus the study, those aspects most likely to yield the most relevant information to the policymaking environment should be selected. For example, in a Senate hearing on the impact of robotics on the U.S. work force, the invited speakers presented testimony on different policy mechanisms (and their support by various constituencies) for minimizing the impact of robotics on the work force (March 18, 1983). The testimony illustrated a concern for the *organizational* and *power* aspects of the social problem. Although the testimony provided information about certain issues, the information that the Senate committee had desired pertained to the *technical* aspects of the social problem; that is, the senators had wanted to know the extent and type of impact on the work force expected before the year 2000. Information on other aspects of the problem were important, the Chairman (Bentsen, D-TX) indicated, but were useless until technical information was available. A research study responding to the Chairman's concern would then develop research questions focused primarily on the technical, rather than organizational, aspects of the robotic work force problem.

Although each of the four foci described above represent different ways of viewing your social problem, your study would ideally provide information on more than one of these aspects. For example, your study might provide technical information appropriate for a range of possible organizational structures.

In addition to focusing on more than one aspect, research questions should recognize that different aspects of the social problem will interact in significant ways (Etzioni, 1979). Therefore, to the extent possible, policy research questions should not only address the effects of each aspect on the problem, but also the effects of aspects on each other. In this way, the policy research results will more likely reflect the reality of the social problem.

Finally, the researcher should be forewarned that exact focus of the social problem may be dictated by the type of impact (see Step 1) that you decided you would like your study to have (Brown, 1982). For example, suppose you decide that your study will have an impact of an incremental nature. Given such a desired impact, aspects of the social problem pertaining to societal consensus will be ignored. This will be true since incremental studies do not attempt to change current values and assumptions about the social problem. Therefore, in making the decisions involved in both the first and second steps, remember that the decisions are interrelated. Research questions stemming from an understanding of this interrelationship will be more reasonable.

Step 3: Identify malleable variables. In completing the first and second steps, decisions about aspects of the social problem to be studied and the type of impact desired will have been made. These decisions will result in a set of variables for the social problem that could be included in the policy research effort. From this set of variables, those that are the most malleable will need to be chosen. Malleable variables are variables that can be changed to improve the social problem. It will be these variables that will be the focus of the research questions formulated. Step 3, then, is the process of assessing the set of variables for their malleability and choosing those that are the most malleable.

Whether or not a variable is malleable depends not only on the extent to which it can be technically changed, but the extent to which society and policymakers want it to be changed. For example, parental child-rearing practices and the distribution of resources to different poverty programs are malleable variables since they can be modified technically and society is typically open to their change.

In contrast to malleable variables are those variables that are static and unalterable (e.g., gender, height). For example, "the moral character of backpackers may be a significant variable in determining crime rates in the wilderness, but unless park or forest service officials can screen [the backpackers] in that way, the knowledge is of no use" (Wildavsky, 1979, p. 217). Therefore, since the moral character of backpackers tends not to be amenable to change, both by society and through technical means, it can be described as a nonmalleable variable.

Since the objective of policy research is to provide policymakers with useful recommendations, policy studies tend to focus primarily on malleable variables. Although nonmalleable variables may be included in the analysis as controls in statistical equations, research conclusions should focus primarily on those variables that can be modified, above and beyond the influence of other factors.

Given the almost exclusive focus on malleable variables, policy researchers must be able to identify, from their lists of variables, those that are most malleable. Such identification necessitates a certain understanding of the social problem and sociopolitical environment—an understanding that the researcher has presumably acquired by this point. Some general guidelines for identifying malleable variables follow.

First, symbolic variables such as attitudes, labels, perceptions, and laws are typically more malleable than natural processes. For example, acid rain may be a function of a variety of different factors, including weather conditions and industrial pollution. Clearly, weather conditions, as natural processes, are not generally amenable to overt change by policymakers. On the other hand, the level of industrial pollution, resulting from inadequate public pressure and laws, is more easily changed. Therefore in selecting variables for focus, those that are symbolic are worth particular attention.

A second guideline in assessing malleability is that narrowly focused variables tend to be more malleable than broadly gauged variables. For example, although resource allocation to schools, parental poverty, and racial discrimination are all important factors affecting a young child's performance in school, only the first factor—resource allocation—has tended to receive a great deal of attention. The other two factors—poverty and discrimination—tend to be so broadly focused as to necessitate a substantial commitment by policymakers to bring about any change at all.

A third guideline is that variables represented as continuous, normal distributions are generally more malleable than variables represented as dichotomous or bimodal distributions. For dichotomous variables, stakeholders become polarized at one of the extremes on the variable, as in the case of whether or not school busing is morally correct. Stakeholders can either agree or disagree with busing; no middle ground is made available. In contrast to dichotomous variables, continuous variables can be viewed in terms of gradations or levels of agreement/disagreement. Such gradations allow opinions and recommendations to be less formative and threatening, making compromises more likely. Examples of continuous variables might be the level of a school system (rather than whether or not full integration is appropriate) or increasing the acceptance of school busing (rather than whether or not full acceptance of busing has been achieved in a particular community).

A fourth guideline is that variables leading to improvements in basic human needs, such as freedom from want or suffering, are generally more malleable than variables that do not deal directly with basic human needs. Variables not concerned with basic needs are less malleable since their importance and utility tend to be questioned more often. For example, Lyle Saunders of the Ford Foundation argues strongly that a country should be persuaded to construct its population policy on the notion that reproduction is a basic human right to be exercised in accordance with private and personal preference. Coupling population policy with a basic human right, then, would yield more international cooperation in family planning, since "this human right is something that both capitalist and communist nations can agree on" (Saunders, 1972, p. 11). In the final analysis, those variables of a social problem concerned with basic human needs should be the long-range focus of the policy researcher. The more effectively researchers can identify these variables, the more likely they are to offer recommendations that can be supported by a majority of the interested parties.

A final guideline for identifying malleable variables is that the malleability of a variable at the start of a research project, may not be the same when the research study ends. For example, in Luis Echeverria's first campaign for president of Mexico in 1969, family planning was denounced as a symbol of U.S. intervention, making family planning services a variable of low malleability (Bergman, 1975). Three years later, in response to new political and economic conditions, President Echeverria reversed his position by announcing the establishment of a nationwide family planning program, thereby increasing the malleability of family planning services. When identifying malleable variables, then, it is important to try to identify those variables that are likely to shift malleability in the future. These variables may either not be included in the analysis or included given the projected shifts.

Step 4: Formulating research questions. In completing the previous steps, the researcher has an idea of the type of impact desired, the aspects of the social problem upon which to focus, and the specific malleable variables to be studied. The research questions should flow easily from this earlier work. Moreover, in the process of formulating the research questions, the researcher should keep in mind Bernard Berelson's (1976) five criteria of research questions most likely to advance public policy:

(1) The research question should address an *important* aspect of the social problem;
(2) the research question should be *do-able*—that is, feasible given expected study constraints;
(3) the research question should be *timely* by providing information that will be useful for current and future decisionmaking;
(4) the research question should provide a *synthesis* of diverse viewpoints so that the results represent an integration to the field, rather than simply an addition; and, last but not least,
(5) the research question should exhibit *policy responsiveness* by addressing issues in a manner that will help policymakers act on the social problem.

In sum, these five criteria are challenging standards for any policy research study. However, by failing to meet these standards, the researcher runs the risk of proceeding with a study for which the results may have questionable utility.

SELECT RESEARCH INVESTIGATORS

The final activity in conceptualizing the research study is the selection of the research investigators. In selecting the investigators, three decisions must be made:

- To conduct the study as a team or solo effort.
- To choose researchers with appropriate disciplinary backgrounds.
- To involve advisors in the study.

Depending on the size of the study, the first two decisions may be pro forma. In small studies, the researcher may be the sole investigator with a given disciplinary background. In large studies, however, the first two decisions may require considerably more judgment. The researcher should determine if the study is best approached as a team effort or done alone. Teams should be preferred if sufficient resources exist, the study can be apportioned into separate tasks, and different perspectives and skills are needed. In such situations, teams can provide innovative and multiple inputs into the research effort, above and beyond the skills or a single researcher. In other situations, however, teams may not be quite as effective. As teams may seriously retard the progress of the study through meetings, disagreements, and the need for compromise, if time is short the study should be conducted as a solo effort (with the aid of assistants) or be divided into separate tasks.

If a team of research investigators is to be used to conduct the study, the disciplinary composition of that team needs to be determined. Some studies should only be approached as a multidisciplinary effort (e.g., a study of labor should include both psychologists and economists). Other studies may be done more efficiently—albeit narrowly—if performed by a team of people with similar, though certainly not identical, disciplinary backgrounds.

The third decision to be made about the research investigators concerns the use of advisors in the research study. Experience as well as systematic study emphasize the utility of advisory panels, steering committees, and task forces in doing policy research (Carter & Kosinski, 1981; Gibbons, 1983; Van de Vall & Bolas, 1982). For example, the success of a study of nursing homes in helping the Michigan governor to decide about adopting a set of new regulations was felt to be directly attributable to the use of a task force of interested citizens (Carter & Kosinski, 1981).

Several reasons have been given for the usefulness of task forces and advisory panels. First, such groups help to create enough ownership among the stakeholders, as members of the panel, to ensure that results of the study are used. Second, the committees help to keep the study on its most reasonable and relevant course. Finally, such committees provide conflicting groups with the opportunity to confront each other directly in an effort to reach compromise.

The use of advisory panels can also create problems, however. For example, delays in study progress while awaiting decisions and increased conflict if panel discussions are not handled properly are possible consequences of using advisory groups. For these reasons, ground rules in the use of advisory panels for a particular study should be established at the outset of the study. The Office of Technology Assessment, for example, only uses advisory panels to critique reports, not to approve them. In this way, delays encountered while the panel tries to decide whether to approve the report are avoided (Gibbons, 1983). Van de Vall and Bolas (1982) suggest using advisory panels primarily at the beginning (e.g., problem definition) and end (e.g., recommendations) of the research study. Delays during the research process will then be held to a minimum. Finally, Carter and Kosinski (1981) recommend the use of a task force only under conditions in which time pressure is acute (to limit dialogue to practical discussions), and the task is seen as necessary, visible, and with the potential to produce useful results. In sum, these suggestions should help the researcher to select an appropriate group of investigators to participate and contribute to a worthwhile and productive policy research effort.

EXERCISES

1. Reexamine Figure 3.1, alternative models describing causes for nutritional deficiencies in ghetto children. What types of stakeholders might support each model? Why? Can you describe an approach for achieving a consensus about the two models?

2. Develop a preliminary model describing possible causes for students dropping out of college. Remember that the model should delineate definitions, assumptions, and values as well as the presumed causes.

3. Suppose you were to do a policy research study that had as its purpose the reduction of college dropouts. Having developed the model in Exercise 2, complete each of the four steps for formulating specific research questions.

4

Technical Analysis

In this chapter the activities involved in the technical analysis of the study are discussed. Guidelines for operationalizing variables, designing study methodology, conducting the analysis, and developing conclusions and tentative recommendations are presented.

Following the preparation and conceptualization of the research study, the next stage in the policy research process is the technical analysis of the social problem. Technical analysis refers to the examination of factors that may cause the social problem. As a result of this analysis, conclusions about causal factors are reached. From these conclusions, recommendations for lessening the impact of those factors on the social problem can then be tentatively advanced.

Technical analysis is the stage in the policy research process involving activities that are the most analogous to those of the traditional research process. Variables are operationalized, the methodology is designed and undertaken, analysis is performed, results obtained, and conclusions drawn. Despite the apparent similarities, though, performing these activities as part of a policy research effort necessitates somewhat different emphases and concerns than when they are performed as part of a traditional research process. For this reason, the technical analysis stage of the policy research process is described in some detail. Specifically, the four major activities are as follows:

(1) operationalization of variables
(2) design of study methodology
(3) conduct of analysis and
(4) development of conclusions and tentative recommendations

OPERATIONALIZATION OF VARIABLES

At this stage in the policy research process, a set of research questions will have been formulated about the influence of selected malleable variables on the social problem. Having set forth the research questions, the policy researcher must now operationalize the malleable variables; that is, define the variables in terms of specific measurable indicators. The variables, as used in the research questions, may be as vague and far-reaching as economic stability, or as narrowly defined as the IQ scores of preschool children. Therefore, the extent to which the variables need to be operationalized will vary depending on the specificity of the research questions.

For every variable that must be operationalized, the researcher should first precisely define that variable, and second, select specific indicators for measuring the variable as defined. For example, in a World Bank study on teacher training in less developed countries (Husen, Saha, & Noonan, 1978), the extent of teacher training needed to be operationalized. The variable was defined by the researchers as the extent of a "teacher's certification or level of competence as determined by 'officially' recognized credentials" (1978, p. 11). From this definition, the following indicators were selected: number of years of schooling attained, possession of a teaching diploma, teaching experience, cognitive ability, and salary.

Although operationalizing variables seems to be a fairly straight forward process, in policy research this process can be riddled with difficulties. First, variables may not be directly measurable. The lack of measurability may be due to several reasons: (a) time constraints on the study (e.g., showing changes in economic stability may take decades rather than months); (b) conceptual nature of the variable (e.g., "racial tolerance" is not easily operationalized); and (c) the political sensitivity of the variable (e.g., extent of illegal immigration from Mexico is not a variable currently amenable to precise measurement).

Second, there may be no single, universally accepted measure of the variable. For example, measuring poverty among the elderly poses special problems (Girshick & Williamson, 1982). For some information users (e.g., the federal government), poverty is defined solely in terms of actual earned income. Other users, however, (e.g., University of Wisconsin's Institute for Research on Poverty) argue that poverty should be measured by adjusting actual income for a variety of nonincome sources of well-being. Such sources might include net worth or human capital. Furthermore, the actual measurement used may be chosen for political reasons. For example, the social security administration has been accused of purposely defining poverty in a way that keeps the numbers of poor low so as to be politically, rather than nutritionally acceptable (Girshick & Williamson, 1982).

A final difficulty with operationalizing variables in policy research may occur because a complex array of different indicators are needed to measure a variable adequately. For example, the effectiveness of a mental health center can be measured by a complex range of indicators, including employee morale, consumer satisfaction, competitive survival and growth of the center, community knowledge and support for the center, improvement in consumer mental health, and the cost efficiency with which services are delivered.

To deal with the difficulties involved in operationalizing variables, the policy researcher has several options available. For variables that are not directly measurable, the policy researcher should consider the use of "proxy" or substitute indicators. Proxy indicators are measures that reasonably substitute for the desired concept. By definition, proxy indicators cannot provide a complete assessment of the variable; nevertheless, their use promotes some partial assessment of the phenomenon of interest. For example, to assess "a community's racial tolerance," proxy indicators might include the unemployment rates of different ethnic groups in the community, a racial attitude survey of randomly selected citizens, the affirmative action policies of corporations in the community, the extent of school and residential voluntary segregation in the community, or ratings by respected community leaders and experts. None of these indicators—alone or together—provides a complete assessment of "racial tolerance." The indicators do provide, however, a partial substitute describing key aspects of the variable.

In using proxy indicators, the researcher must remember the limitations that their use imposes on conclusions to be drawn from the research. For example, if racial tolerance is measured solely by the unemployment rates of ethnic subgroups, conclusions are limited to a fairly narrow interpretation of tolerance. Recommendations, therefore, will need to argue persuasively for applying the results to a broader concept of tolerance.

Another way to overcome difficulties in operationalizing variables is to use multiple indicators for each concept (e.g., Campbell, 1969). The use of multiple indicators promotes research studies that are multidimensional in nature. Furthermore, multiple indicators allow for the examination of different types of effects attributable to causal factors. A study using only single indicators runs the risk of yielding little new insight by having only null relationships to report. Finally, the use of multiple indicators has the additional advantage of allowing for the inclusion of indicators that are preferred by proponents of conflicting models of the social problem. For example, environmental quality could be measured by economic variables for stakeholders who view pollution as a question of economics, by health standards for stakeholders interested in quality, and by subjective aesthetic ratings for stakeholders who value the environment for its beauty and aesthetic appeal. Given this range of perspectives on environmental quality, a study on such an issue could enhance its appeal and credibility to a wide audience of users if indicators pertaining to each perspective were included in the study.

Given the potential difficulties in operationalizing variables, the selection of indicators should be done with great care and thought (see, for example, Edwards [in press] in this series for a detailed discussion of scale validity and reliability). Indicators should provide the closest approximation to the variable as possible. When the indicators deviate in some way from the original definition of the variable (as with the use of proxy indicators), the extent to which these deviations will affect the outcome of the study should be thoroughly understood. This understanding will be needed when you as the researcher must present the results and recommendations of the study.

DESIGN OF STUDY METHODOLOGY

At its best, policy research is a matter of trade-offs and compromises. Because they address the sometimes ambitious questions of decisionmakers rather than of academicians, policy researchers frequently find themselves at the fringes of existing social science methodology—adapting, combining, and improvising as they go. (Smith & Robbins, 1982, p.45)

Because policy research operates at the boundaries of research methodology, there is no single, comprehensive methodology for doing the technical analysis of policy research (Coleman, 1975). Without the constraints imposed by a singular methodological approach, policy researchers have been free to pursue a variety of methodological directions in technically analyzing social problems. For example, in a review of 300 policy research studies, Pamela Doty (1983) identified two divergent methodological approaches for doing policy research. The first approach, which she terms the moral/philosophical approach, is characterized by "think pieces" that selectively pull together and synthesize theoretical literature, data, and existing research findings from a variety of sources in support of an argument or thesis. In contrast to the moral/philosophical approach is the empirical approach, which emphasizes collection and analysis of data rather than interpretive synthesis. Although these approaches need not be mutually exclusive, studies that incorporate both approaches are rare.

The dichotomy of methodological approaches characterized by Doty is particularly noteworthy since it serves to remind the researcher that technical analysis involves far more than the simple collection and analysis of quantitative data. Argument and rational scrutiny of information are equally as important elements in the technical analysis of the social problem (Majone, 1980). In fact, Doty (1983) raises the important issue that we, as empirically based social science researchers, must all face. To paraphrase her: Instead of asking what is the appropriate method for conducting policy-relevant scientific research, perhaps we should first ask whether social policy research must be scientific research at all; that is, can policy research also include a discourse on values, goals, and assumptions? To a researcher trained in traditional research methods, a discourse is unacceptable. In contrast, a policy researcher functioning in an environment less susceptible to scientific control must consider such alternative methods.

Methods for Technical Analysis

Since no comprehensive methodology for policy research exists, researchers must know a variety of different methods in order to apply them selectively to particular research questions. In this section, a sampling of some of the methods that can be used in policy research are briefly presented. The reader should understand that not all methods are appropriate for every research study context or question. For example, some of the methods depend on already existing information (e.g., focused synthesis). Those methods may be most appropriate when time is short and existing information is reliable. Other methods involve data collection (e.g., surveys). These methods tend to be most appropriate when new information is needed to generate new policy options. Finally, some of the methods are most appropriate when alternative policy options exist (e.g., cost-benefit/ cost-effectiveness analyses). These methods help to select the optimal policy among the evaluated alternatives.

Focused synthesis. One method of doing policy research has been referred to as "focused synthesis" (Doty, 1982). An example of focused synthesis is offered in a study for AID (Agency for International Development) on the rural water supply problems in developing countries (Burton, 1979). This policy research effort was

> based upon a survey of recent available and accessible literature; on my own field experience in the past five years in Africa and Latin America; and on discussions with individuals at the Ross Institute, International Reference Centre for Community Water Supply in The Hague, the World Health Organization, and the British Ministry for Overseas Development. (Burton, 1979, p. iv)

Findings from a synthesis of these information sources yielded several policy recommendations for improving the water supply of developing countries' rural communities.

Focused synthesis is somewhat akin to traditional literature reviews by involving the selective review of written materials and existing research findings relevant to the particular research questions. However, focused synthesis differs from traditional literature reviews by discussing information obtained from a variety of sources beyond published articles. For example, a typical synthesis might include discussions with experts and stakeholders, congressional hearings, anecdotal stories, personal past experience of the researchers, unpublished documents, staff memoranda, and published materials.

Another way that focused synthesis differs from traditional literature review is in its purpose. Literature reviews tend simply to describe sets of research studies and identify gaps or areas needing more research. Occasionally, methods such as meta-analysis (see Rosenthal, 1984, in this series) or the synthesis itself may be done less formally (e.g., using deductive reasoning). While focused synthesis will generally describe its sources, information sources are used only to the extent to which they directly contribute to the overall synthesis.

A final way in which focused syntheses and literature reviews differ is in the extent to which they stand alone. Most traditional literature reviews are used as precursors or background for later research. Gaps identified by review are presumably filled by a subsequent data collection effort. In contrast, focused synthesis tends to be used alone in a technical analysis. The results of the synthesis *are* the results of the policy research effort. The recommendations presented are derived exclusively from the synthesized information, with no primary data collected. Since the recommendations are based solely on the information used in the focused synthesis, such a policy research effort is constrained by both the availability and timeliness of the information. Nevertheless, focused synthesis provides an advantage over other methods in that it can be performed in an efficient and opportune fashion.

Secondary analysis. Another method that uses existing information is referred to here as secondary analysis. This method is, by far, the most cost-efficient method for answering policy research questions.

Secondary analysis refers to the analysis and reanalysis of existing databases. Such analysis may involve a variety of statistical procedures, as appropriate. For example, Don Campbell (1969) describes an analysis of traffic fatalities in Connecticut over a nine-year period. By obtaining and analyzing public records on accidents, the researchers were able to determine the effects of a new "crackdown" on speeding.

The variation in statistical procedures ranges from the assessment of very simple two-variable relationships to the modeling of complex behavior projected into the future. An example of the latter type of analysis was done by Reutlinger and Selowsky (1976). As part of their study, they obtained data on individuals' daily calorie consumption. With these data, they developed sophisticated econometric forecasting models to assess the current and projected nature and magnitude of undernutrition.

Secondary analyses are possible, of course, only when the proper databases are available. Proper databases may be difficult to obtain if the social problem has only recently been recognized (e.g., acid rain), if the problem is immensely unacceptable to society (e.g., incest), or the problem is so political or complex that the accuracy of databases is questionable (e.g., tax evasion). In such situations, it may still be possible to do a secondary analysis by building a new database of selected items taken from a combination of different databases. If such databases construction cannot be accomplished, other policy research methods may need to be considered.

Field experiments. One method for collecting primary data on the social problem is to conduct a field experiment. In a field experiment, some type of intervention (or interventions) is developed to alleviate the social problem. The intervention is then implemented into the target population for a while and data on resulting changes are collected. For example, Paul and Gross (1981) conducted a field experiment on employees of the city of San Diego, California (cited in Guizzo & Bondy, 1983). The purpose of the experiment was to test the utility of organization development techniques for increasing employee morale and productivity. The intervention consisted of personal interviews, team building workshops, counseling, process consultation, and training in management skills. By comparing the productivity and morale of employees receiving the intervention with comparable employees not receiving the intervention, the researchers were able to confirm the positive effects of the intervention on employees.

There are essentially two types of field experiments: those that are randomized and those that are not (termed quasi-experiments). A randomized field experiment attempts to mirror the requirements of a laboratory experiment. These requirements necessitate the use of control groups, pretest and posttest measures of variables, and the random assignment of people or units to different conditions in which they are either exposed to the intervention or serve as controls.

When designed and implemented properly, randomized field experiments can provide valuable information on the causes of social problems. As a result of the experiment, the researcher knows exactly what the intervention caused or failed to cause. Nevertheless, the random assignment of people or units to different conditions is not always possible in policy research.

Quasi-experiments offer an alternative to randomized experiments for testing the effects of an intervention on a social problem. The differences between quasi- and randomized experiments are that individuals or units are not randomly assigned, control groups are not necessarily used, and both pretest and posttest measures are not always taken. By eliminating these features of randomized experiments, the researcher loses the ability to distinguish clearly cause from effect. Nevertheless, much is still learned from quasi-experiments. Furthermore, quasi-experiments are particularly useful when there are limits on the data availability, when time is an issue, or when matched (or no) comparison groups provide a more justifiable and less costly alternative to randomized controls. There are many different varieties of quasi-experiments such as regression discontinuity designs, time series designs, and staged implementation designs. Campbell (1969) and Cook and Campbell (1979) provide excellent descriptions of these varieties.

A final issue to consider in doing field experiments is that policy research must not only explain existing societal conditions but project future conditions as well. This projection into the future may be difficult if an experiment is conducted under conditions that are so dynamic that the results are contrained to the particular period of experimentation. In such situations, alternative methods for conducting the policy research effort are probably more appropriate.

Qualitative methods. Qualitative information gathering is used in both case studies and focused synthesis. In addition, there are several other qualitative methods for gathering primary data (Patton, 1980). The use of focus groups (Calder, 1977) is one such technique in which selected individuals are gathered in a group and guided into a focused discussion on prespecified topics. Such groups are excellent for generating issues and exploring potential causal factors. Another qualitative method—in-depth interviews—are one-on-one, semistructured interviews with selected individuals. Copious notes are usually taken during the interviews and analyzed later. Finally, participant observation, which involves the investigator serving both as a participant and observer in gathering information on an ongoing process (e.g., an emergency ward at a public hospital), can provide valuable insight into causal factors and preliminary findings. It should be noted that none of these qualitative methods alone can yield "conclusive" results; however, they do provide valuable information that more rigorous methods may overlook.

Surveys. Another method for gathering primary data on the social problem and its causes is through surveys (see Fowler, 1984, in this series, for more detail). Surveys can vary in scope, content, and rigor. For example, a survey may involve a series of qualitative interviews with a small number of purposefully selected individuals (see Patton, 1980, for more information). Or the survey may be quite extensive and time-consuming involving scientifically selected samples to minimize the margin of error. Surveys may also differ in terms of the data collection method used. Data collection may involve personal interviews or written questionnaires administered at one time or over several time periods to selected individuals or selected members of a unit (e.g., household, community, state).

Due to the great variety in survey methodologies, the policy researcher contemplating a survey should design it carefully. Such issues as access to the sample population, question wording, feasibility of administration, time, and cost must be carefully considered prior to undertaking such an effort. Given these considerations, the policy researcher will frequently find that only fairly small, purposefully sampled surveys are feasible in the policy arena. Furthermore, unless the surveys are administered to the same sample over time to ascertain changes in variables of interest, conclusions about the causes of the social problem may be difficult to make. Nevertheless, surveys (even small ones) may provide useful input for the policymaking arena.

Case studies. Another method for collecting primary data is the case study. Case studies tend to be a frequently used policy research method as they are usually quick, cost efficient, and allow room for impressionistic analyses of a situation. As argued by Rist (1982), case studies also have several other contributions. Case studies allow for the identification of behaviors and other variables that were not expected to be related to the social problem. They provide for a more in-depth analysis of superficial statistical portrayals of populations (e.g., Do women who have abortions suffer irreparable emotional damage, as President Reagan's "statistics" would have us believe?). They provide for a more complete understanding of a situation's complexity by examining behavior in context. Case studies also promote examination of the process by which an intervention or policy action has been implemented (e.g., how was a congressional policy action changed as it was interpreted and adapted by federal government agencies, state government agencies, and, finally, the local service delivery program). This last contribution of case studies is particularly useful for developing recommendations concerning the future implementation of policy options.

Most case studies tend to be qualitative in nature; however, this need not always be true. For example, observations or diaries can be kept that systematically quantify the numbers of different types of behaviors occurring during specified periods of time. Cain, Khanam, and Nahar (1979) conducted such a case study on the ways in which household members allocated their time. (For guidance in quantifying approaches to case studies, see Yin, 1984, in this series.)

Cost-benefit and cost-effectiveness analyses. Cost benefit analyses refer to the set of methods by which a researcher compares the costs and benefits to society of alternative policy options. Conceptually, cost-benefit analysis is a cornerstone of policy research providing for the identification of policy options that are likely to yield the most benefits at the least cost.[1] In reality, however, the costs and benefits of different policy options are rarely so clearly identified or understood to allow for their explicit analysis. Nevertheless, cost-benefit analysis is a method useful to policy research efforts and should be applied when possible.

In its purest form, cost-benefit analysis involves a comparison of the monetary value of benefits attributable to a policy option with the monetary value of costs (see Levin, 1975). By calculating costs and benefits in terms of a common yardstick (e.g., monetary value), comparisons of the relative attractiveness of alternatives (i.e., in terms of rates of return on investment, benefit-to-cost ratios, and so on) can be easily performed.

An example of a cost-benefit analysis used in policy research is described by Henry Levin (1975) for the evaluation of water resource projects. Costs associated with water resource projects, such as dam construction and maintenance, could be readily measured in monetary terms. Furthermore, such benefits as hydroelectric power and water for agriculture could also be assigned monetary values. Therefore, in determining which of a number of different possible water resource projects to undertake, a government agency could simply rank them according to their benefit-to-cost ratios and start at the top.

Despite the apparent simplicity of such an approach, cost-benefit analysis can rarely be applied to policy research problems. The difficulty lies with valuation of benefits in monetary terms. Most benefits resulting from policy options cannot be valued monetarily. For example, what are the monetary values of reduced child abuse, fair housing practices, less social alienation, better schools, or fewer nursing home deaths? While these policies clearly have positive benefits, a consensus on the monetary value of these benefits would be difficult to achieve. Therefore, for such policies, cost-benefit analyses are usually replaced by cost-effectiveness analyses (Thompson, 1980).

In cost-effectiveness analyses, the monetary costs of a policy option are still computed. However, the benefits of the policy are expressed in terms of its actual or expected outcome. For example, cost-effectiveness ratios of the following types may be seen:

- the number of dollars needed for an alcohol abuser to achieve abstinence;
- the number of dollars needed for a former convict to not recidivate;
- the number of dollars needed to achieve a certain percentage increase in the literacy rate of the population; or
- the number of dollars needed to reduce infant mortality by a certain percentage.

In constructing cost-effectiveness ratios, one should note that the ratios say little about whether the policy should or should not be implemented. Without another ratio against which to compare, a cost-effectiveness ratio has little meaning. Furthermore, even with a comparison ratio, a policy option may not be judged by policymakers to be *sufficiently* effective to warrant its cost (Thompson et al., 1981).

For both the cost-benefit and cost-effectiveness analyses, costs are assessed for similar variables. Costs tend to include direct costs (e.g., personnel, facilities), indirect costs (e.g., to nonparticipants), and opportunity costs (i.e., what would have been achieved if the resources had been used differently). A problem with assessing costs in this fashion is that nonmonetary costs tend to be ignored. As a result, alternative methods for assessing the costs and benefits of policy options have been devised.

One alternative group of methods for assessing costs and benefits of policy options includes Social Impact Assessment (SIA) and Environmental Impact Statements (Finsterbusch & Motz, 1980). The purpose of these approaches is to measure the range of impacts on people, groups, organizations, and communities that will result from one or a set of policy options. An example of an SIA for the Chicago Crosstown Expressway is described by Finsterbusch and Motz (1980). In analyzing the impact of the expressway, a variety of costs were studied, including aesthetics, traffic, directness of route, in addition to the more traditional construction and maintenance costs. To assess benefits, potential impacts on employment, urban renewal, and property values were considered.

To ensure that costs and benefits are measured on a common scale, each variable is typically assigned a subjective score of acceptability; that is, for each impact a score is assigned indicating how acceptable a particular impact is to those involved in the policy action. While this score is hardly as defensible as monetary value, the added validity of such an assessment, by considering a range of costs and benefits, makes SIAs a valuable method for policy research.

Another alternative for assessing costs and benefits involves decision-analytic approaches to evaluation (MacRae, 1980; Nagel, 1975). Decision-analytic approaches allow particular benefits and costs to be assigned any numeric score on any common dimension by any number of experts. The numeric scores might represent such dimensions as importance to the population at large or likelihood of benefit or cost occurring. With such numeric scores, statistically expected values of each policy option can be computed. Comparing these values for each option will then yield the optimal policy. These methods, which include multiattribute utility analysis (Edwards, Guttentag, & Snapper, 1975) and cost-optimization procedures (Nagel, 1975), are much too complex to describe here. Suffice to say that they are one method for assessing benefits and costs.

In sum, policy research encompasses a number of different methods for undertaking the technical analysis. A policy research study may rely exclusively on a focused synthesis of available information sources or on surveys in which primary collection of quantitative data may be performed. Qualitative data may be felt to be more important, necessitating the use of case studies or qualitative methods, or an actual intervention may be constructed and implemented, involving a randomized or quasi-experiment. Existing data may be available, permitting the use of secondary analysis. Finally, the study may focus more precisely on the costs and benefits of alternative policy options, involving the use of cost benefit or cost effectiveness approaches to policy research.

Guidelines for Designing Technical Methodology

Apparent from the list of methods described above, the policy researcher has an overwhelming array to choose from in designing a methodology for the study. Therefore, several guidelines for designing a study methodology are offered below.

First, an ideal policy research study is one that combines a number of different research methods, such as survey with focused synthesis, or case study with secondary analysis. An ideal combination is to use both qualitative and quantitative methods (see Smith & Seashore-Louis, 1982, for examples). Such a combination provides several advantages by (a) increasing the perceived validity of the study when the two methods yield corroborating results and (b) providing additional insight that one method alone could not provide.

A second guideline for designing a methodology is that policy research is an empirico-inductive process, interacting with the social problem in striving for a solution. Therefore, rather than posing a "frontal attack on the problem," the methodology should allow for "its routine adaptation to the problem-solving interaction" (Lindblom & Cohen, 1979, p. 61). This implies, then, that policy research methodologies need not be precisely planned out in advance; room for adaptation should be allowed.

A third guideline is that policy researchers should be careful not to "structure an issue merely to fit a 'pet' [research] technique in their kit bags" (House & Coleman, 1980, p. 194). The methodology should be based on the research question, rather than the research question reformulated to fit a preferred methodology.

A fourth guideline is that, because of the time and resource constraints of typical policy research studies, developing original instruments and engaging in primary data collection of a rigorous nature should be avoided when possible. As pointed out in the text on secondary research in this series (Stewart, 1984), the amount of data that is publicly available is overwhelming. If the focus of a policy research study can be slightly modified in order to use existing data, such a change may be a worthwhile one. Not only is the use of existing data cost efficient, but when the existing data involve generally accepted instruments (e.g., such social indicators as the cost-of-living and unemployment indices), the perceived validity of the study is enhanced. Researchers who collect data using original instruments must constantly defend their instruments to critics and study users.

A final guideline for designing a methodology for a policy research effort is that the methodology should reflect the sociopolitical environment in which the study is taking place. The methodological design should be responsive to criticisms about study validity, opinions of study users about the design, volatility of the political climate, and potential future changes in social conditions which might affect study conclusions. Four ways to design methodology to respond to its environment are suggested.

One way to conduct an environmentally responsive study is to design a set of several relatively independent substudies, each linked to different scientific and political priorities (Louis, 1982). For example, in 1972, Abt Associates Inc., a contract research firm, undertook a seven-year policy research study of the Rural Experimental Schools (ES) Program (Herriott, 1982). The study had multiple agendas that were expected to change in the future as the ES Program and its sponsor (National Institute of Education) became increasingly under attack in the mid-1970s. Specifically designed to cope with this complexity, the study consisted of six major substudies, each with a highly distinctive research mode (ranging from quantitative to qualitative) and analytic focus (ranging from the individual pupil to the entire program). The six substudies are presented in Table 4.1. Each substudy has a separate budget and staff although some cross-study coordination was undertaken. In developing a design of this nature, the study could be responsive to changing political priorities without repeated disruption.

Another way to design a methodology that responds to its environment is to discuss the design with study users, the sponsor, and/or the study's advisory panel. Criticisms of the design by such individuals provide valuable insight into how it will be received by study stakeholders, and can then help in making design improvements.

A third way of taking the environment into account in the methodological design is to formally predict potential future changes to the environment and the potential impact of these changes on study findings. For example, prior to undertaking a policy research study about community-based care of the elderly, the researcher should be fully aware of the political climate surrounding the issue. If it is possible that care for the elderly may become, in the short run, a politically volatile issue with resulting legislation, the study should be designed to address this possibility. When the political cli-

TABLE 4.1
Substudies Used in the Abt Experimental School (ES)
Policy Research Study

(1) *History study*. A set of structured social and educational histories of each of the ten rural school districts from the founding of their communities through their selection in June 1972 as "ES sites," supplemented by a series of cross-district historical and demographic analyses.

(2) *Case studies*. A set of ten autonomous and unstructured ethnographic case studies analyzing each ES project in the context of its school system, community, and broader sociocultural environment.

(3) *Community study*. An integration of demographic, survey, and field-based observation to consider the interaction of ES project and community context across the ten ES sites.

(4) *Organization study*. An integration of survey questionnaires and field-based observation to describe the ES projects at each site and to explore reasons for variation in project planning, design, implementation, and persistence beyond the period of federal funding.

(5) *Pupil study*. An integration of survey questionnaires, study adapted standardized tests, and commercially prepared tests to explore the impact of participation in the ES program upon pupil cognitive and affective behavior.

(6) *Special Research studies*. Initially unspecified additional studies that eventually consisted of (a) a survey of the information needs and program priorities of rural educators and policymakers, (b) a sociological case study of the implementation of the ES program at the federal level, (c) five structured mini-case studies of ES projects, (d) a cross-case analysis of the eight completed case studies, and (e) a synthesis of the major findings across all substudies of the Rural study.

mate shifts in the predicted fashion, the study will be ready with relevant data.

A final way to design an environmentally sensitive study is to focus on those variables that are insensitive enough to short-term environmental shifts to be stable for the duration of the study and its use. A study on teenage pregnancy that focuses on solutions other than abortion is more likely to remain useful as the power of the Right to Life groups waxes and wanes.

The five guidelines offered here will aid in designing a relevant and appropriate methodology for technically analyzing the social problem. Once the methodology is designed, the researcher will be able to carry it out in as efficient a manner as possible. Following the acquisition of the information (qualitative and/or quantitative) and its analysis, the researcher is ready, first to present the results and conclusions, and, second, to develop tentative policy recommendations. Guidelines for engaging in these two activities comprise the remainder of this chapter.

RESULTS AND CONCLUSIONS

In the process of obtaining results and conclusions from the collected information, the researcher exerts substantial control. As more information is typically gathered than can be communicated quickly to the decision-makers, the researcher must decide which data are to analyzed and in what way. Several suggestions are offered here to help policy researchers obtain results and conclusions most likely to draw policy attention.

An initial suggestion is to structure the results so that they can be presented as simply as possible. Although study users will typically want to know enough about the study results to be able to evaluate them critically the users will not generally know much about statistics. Therefore, the researcher must obtain results that are easily understood by "lay people." This can be done in one of two ways, depending on the complexity of the research questions. First, the researcher can decide to conduct only easily understood analyses, such as cross-tabulations, t-tests, and correlations. Results obtained by such methods can usually be explained easily to most people.

In addition to the use of t-tests and correlations, however, there may be times when more sophisticated statistical procedures (e.g., log-linear analysis, multivariate analysis of variance, Box-Jenkins time series, or LISREL causal modeling) are needed to understand the complex interrelationships of the variables. In such a situation, the results should first be analyzed using the more sophisticated procedures. The major findings from this analysis can then be resubmitted to simpler analysis. For example, using a sophisticated statistical technique such as log-linear regression modeling, you find that two dichotomous variables out of twelve explain an individual's decision to obtain food stamps. Rather than terminating the analysis at this point, you should resubmit the two significant variables along with the dependent variable to a series of cross-tabulations that can be more easily explained and understood than the log-linear analysis. Of course, you should probably mention that the log-linear analysis was done, but the results that are presented need not be so complex.

A second suggestion in using results and conclusions is to evaluate both the political and statistical significance of every analytic finding obtained. Unless the finding is both politically and statistically significant, it is probably not worth noting.

To assess the statistical significance of a finding, researchers must establish significance levels they believe indicate credible and replicable findings. In setting this level, they need not be bound by the traditional .05 alpha level. Since the subject matter of policy research is usually complex and poorly understood, findings may be statistically significant even if a .05 level of significance is not obtained. In certain studies, findings that hold in 85 percent or 90 percent of the cases may be sufficiently robust for policy purposes.

In addition to assessing statistical significance, researchers need to assess the political significance of their findings. Findings are politically significant if they indicate a result that warrants policy action. Findings that are statistically significant need not be politically significant. For example, suppose you find that children using fluoride have fewer cavities (at the .05 level of significance) than children not using fluoride. Now suppose that this difference between the two groups of children actually translates into one-tenth of one less cavity per year. In other words, it would take ten years of using fluoride before a child has one fewer cavity. This finding may not be significant enough to be worth political action given the political costs associated with action. Therefore, findings that are both politically and statistically significant should be emphasized. In assessing political significance of a finding, researchers will need to rely on their own political experience or those of the stakeholders.

A third suggestion for using results and conclusions is that statements of results should be accompanied by a limit of confidence (i.e., a confidence interval). Confidence intervals refer to the range within which a particular statistic is to be believed. In addition to assigning confidence limits to statements of results, the researcher should use other means of quantifying levels of confidence for a result as possible. For example, if the research questions involve comparisons among alternative options or actions, results could specify how much better one option is than another. Of course, any such quantification may be somewhat subjective; however, such statements are much more easily assimilated and remembered than more narrative and complicated comparisons.

A fourth suggestion for using results and conclusions has been viewed by some as an ethical issue. In a proposed list of ethical principles for policy researchers, Stuart Nagel suggests the following principle:

> Policy [researchers] have an obligation to subject their [conclusions] to a sensitivity analysis, whereby they determine how those [conclusions] would change with various changes in the input data, values, assumptions, measurements, sampling, or analysis with which they are working. (1982, p. 433)

This ethical principle implies that policy researchers should take time to reflect on their results and conclusions so that limitations and lack of generalizability across different situations and methods are clearly understood. Such an analysis would seem to be extremely useful, especially if study conclusions intend generalizations beyond the immediate situation in which the data were gathered and analyzed.

A final suggestion for using results is that, when a study has yielded several different findings, each of which support the study conclusions, the policy researcher should primarily emphasize those results that are most acceptable to the audience. For example, Stuart Nagel (1983) describes a policy decision (at the U.S. Supreme Court level) that was intended to eliminate discrimination against women by juries. The case presented to the U.S. Supreme Court concerned the constitutionality of state laws allowing women to be more easily excused from juries than men. A key research study found that the extent of women representation on juries was related to discrimination. However, due to the controversial nature of such a finding, these results were never used as supporting evidence. Instead, the straightforward finding that women are underrepresented on juries in relation to their proportion in the general population was felt to be much more useful information for supporting the conclusion.

It should be noted that this last suggestion refers only to situations where the researcher has findings which all lead to the same conclusion. When the researcher has conflicting or inconsistent findings, reasons for such inconsistency should be identified and appropriate conclusions generated. Although a study failing to yield conclusive results is of little use to the policy arena, a study that makes inaccurate conclusions seriously damages the credibility of policy research far beyond the damage wrought by inconclusive studies.

Apparent from these suggestions for using results and conclusions is that researchers have substantial discretion in selecting results from which conclusions and recommendations will be reached. This discretion needs to be used cautiously and carefully to maintain both study validity and relevance.

DEVELOPING TENTATIVE POLICY RECOMMENDATIONS

Based on the results and conclusions of the technical analysis and the policy researcher's understanding of the sociopolitical environment, tentative policy options are developed. These options describe actions that can be taken at a policy level, given the conclusions of the study. For example, stemming from an experimental study of the Family Assistance Plan (a proposed legislation for guaranteed annual income to poor families), several recommendations for the legislation were developed (Boeckmann, 1976). These recommendations included the following:

(1) Guaranteed income should be totally federalized;
(2) legislation should incorporate Food Stamp Program provisions; and
(3) calculation of income payments should be adjusted for short-term fluctuations in family incomes.

In developing tentative policy recommendations, sources of information other than the research conclusions should be used. Specifically, the researcher should use the knowledge of the sociopolitical context that was acquired while preparing for the policy research study. Supplementing this initial knowledge will be the additional information about the context that has been acquired throughout the course of the technical analysis. By the completion of the analysis, then, the policy researcher will have gained considerable knowledge about the context in which the conclusions will be applied. This knowledge is used to develop tentative recommendations that are both politically and culturally appropriate.

The objective of policy research is to provide policymakers with several different options to help alleviate the social problem. As Don Campbell espouses, the key to an experimenting society is that researchers "make explicit that a given problem solution is only one of several that a policymaker could advocate" (1969, p. 410). In support of this objective, then, developed recommendations should concern different policy actions that can be pursued. For example, recommendations for ameliorating the acid rain problem should not only focus on one solution, such as reducing industrial output. Alternative or supplementary actions stemming from the conclusions should also be recommended.

In addition, alternative recommendations in terms of timing can be proposed (e.g., activities that could be done immediately in addition to those to be done in the distant future can be recommended). Finally, the recommendations can provide alternatives in terms of the policy mechanisms to be used. For example, ways of solving a social problem through administrative regulations as well as the allocation of resources can both be proposed. It is only by suggesting a range of different types of actions that policymakers will be able to select those options that most adequately conform to the needs of the political arena.

In this section, we have discussed the development of *tentative* policy recommendations. The recommendations are considered tentative at this point, because they stem primarily from research conclusions and secondarily from information on the sociopolitical climate gathered in a relatively casual, nonsystematic fashion. Although most research stops at this point and presents these tentative policy options as final recommendations, we strongly believe that the policy researcher's task is not over yet. A more systematic assessment of the political environment is necessary to determine the precise feasibility of the various options initially offered.

In addition to determining the feasibility of recommendations, it is only by fully understanding the political environment that the policy researcher can offer suggestions for rallying support behind policy options. In the past, researchers have passively accepted the political environment as unchangeable. In so doing, however, the researcher risks the possibility that the environment will not support implementation of any of the recommendations. To minimize this possibility, we suggest that policy researchers couple the recommendations stemming from their research with suggestions for modifying the political environment to support the recommendations. We believe that it is only by providing these suggestions that the policy options will be appropriately implemented and solutions to social problems forthcoming. In the following chapter, activities involved in analyzing the environment to yield implementable recommendations are discussed.

EXERCISES

1. List some indicators and proxy measures of the following variables:
   • environmental quality
   • quality of education in public schools
   • racial tolerance of a community
   • quality of life of welfare recipients

2. Prepare a large piece of paper with the following table on it, and then fill in the blank cells.

	Advantages	Disadvantages
Focused synthesis		
Secondary analysis		
Field experiments		
Qualitative methods		
Surveys		
Case studies		
Cost-benefit/ cost-effectiveness analysis		

3. Choose five combinations of the seven methods described in this chapter (e.g., field experiments and case studies). For each combination, describe general situations in which you would want to use such a combination, a specific example, advantages, and potential difficulties.

4. List five difficulties of doing cost-benefit analyses in policy research. For each difficulty, describe at least one way in which that difficulty can be overcome.

NOTE

1. I thank Stuart Nagel for his comments in this regard on earlier drafts of the manuscript.

5

Analysis of Study Recommendations

The analysis of study recommendations is discussed in this chapter. Included in this discussion are analysis of implementation parameters; assessment of the potential consequences of recommendations; estimation of the probability that the recommendations will be adequately implemented; and preparation of final recommendations.

Stemming from the results of the technical analysis, a set of conclusions and tentative policy recommendations have been developed that are expected to help alleviate the social problem. Given the work thus far, the policy researcher will feel fairly certain that the policy recommendations will effectively achieve their intended goals, if implemented properly. However, "merely saying that something should be done—without saying how—is an abdication of responsibility" for which social scientists are frequently guilty (Wildavsky, 1979, p. 126). In the words of Paul Bachrach:

> One oversight that has impeded the social scientist in his struggle to solve issues of overpopulation, urban decay, etc. has been, in my view, an insufficient attention to the political power . . . Social scientists have failed to seriously consider the formulation of a public policy issue and the nature of the recommended solution as a *means* to generate and marshal commitment, public support, and power resources of potential or existing groups that, if properly motivated, would be instrumental in bringing about sufficient change in the distribution of power to secure the adoption of a meaningful government policy. . . . For the analyst, to neglect to carefully examine political strategy as an integral part of his problem is to fail his responsibility as a scholar. (1972, pp. 15-17)

In developing study recommendations, then, the following basic rule of policy research must be considered: *Unless the sociological, political, and organizational contexts are explicitly taken into account in developing policy recommendations, the recommendations probably will not be sufficiently implemented to achieve the desired results.*

An example of a policy recommendation that did not take this basic rule into account is the policy forwarded in the early 1970s to deal with the problem of inadequate living conditions for the poor (Nagel, 1983). The policy recommended a homeownership program for the poor that involved government guaranteed mortgages at low interest rates. The policy action was expected to increase poor people's self-esteem by owning a home, encouraging greater care given to the dwellings, and creating a happier, more productive community. Instead of these desired outcomes, the program failed. Although numerous reasons can be advanced for the program's failure, one reason stands out. The policy failed to consider the context in which the program was implemented. By using the private-sector real estate industry, incentives clashed. Real estate agents wanted houses to be sold quickly and at inflated costs, while the poor needed houses at lower costs accompanied with the time and aid to make wise investment decisions. Without government intervention to protect the poor, the program could hardly be expected to succeed. Therefore, if this sociological context had been considered prior to policy action, a more successful program may have been implemented.

To ensure that study recommendations reflect sociopolitical as well as technical considerations, activities for analyzing study recommendations are included as an essential stage in the policy research process. These activities are undertaken following the technical analysis, rather than prior, since at this point a credible basis for the recommendations has been provided by the technical data. While modifications to the recommendations may be needed to ensure implementation, at least the basis for the recommendations can be tied to empirical research. Nevertheless, if desired, miniversions of the analysis described in this chapter can be done earlier on to achieve an understanding of feasible recommendations.

The activities involved in an analysis of study recommendations include the following:

(1) analysis of implementation parameters involved in study recommendations;
(2) assessment of potential consequences of recommendations;
(3) estimation of the probability that recommendations will be adequately implemented; and
(4) preparation of final recommendations.

A discussion of each of these activities comprises the remainder of this chapter.

ANALYSIS OF IMPLEMENTATION PARAMETERS

In order to ensure that policy recommendations are feasible and acceptable, an analysis of the *stakeholders* and *organizational parameters* involved in the implementation of each recommendation should be done. The information for conducting such an analysis will need to be collected through fairly structured interviews with stakeholders, subject matter experts, individuals with previous relevant experience, and agents potentially responsible for implementation. The interviews should be structured to obtain information on the parameters as described in detail below.

Analysis of Stakeholders

As discussed in Chapter 1, a characteristic of policymaking is that, at any given time, public policy is the equilibrium or compromise between conflicting interests. That is, "policy moves in the direction desired by the groups gaining influence and away from the desires of groups losing influence" (Dye, 1978, p. 24). As a result, then, an essential parameter influencing the likelihood that a recommendation will be implemented is the power structure of stakeholders involved in the recommendation. By conducting an analysis of the power structure, the policy researcher attempts to answer the question: Under what conditions would a majority of the powerful stakeholders accept the proposed recommendation?

To conduct a stakeholder analysis, the researcher begins with the list of stakeholders developed as part of the preparatory activities (see Chapter 2). To this list are added other stakeholders identified while conceptualizing the study and conducting the technical analysis. At this point, the list may be fairly long. For example, Larry Wade (1972) compiled a list of 51 organizations sufficiently opposed to a street and road tax in California to contribute to a political campaign. The organizations ranged from an asphalt service company providing $125 to Shell Oil's contribution of $50,000. Despite the numerous organizations on Wade's list, decisionmakers, proponents of the tax, affected citizens, and interested groups who did not contribute campaign funds were not even included.

Since any policy researcher's list of stakeholders compiled earlier in the policy research process will probably be as unmanageably long as Wade's list, the list should be reduced if possible. The list can be reduced either by grouping stakeholders in terms of similar attitudes and motives, or by narrowing the list to only those stakeholders with the strongest interests (e.g., as defined by the size of their campaign contribution). Once the list of stakeholders has been reduced, the next step is to distinguish between those stakeholders who are *responsible* for the final decision to implement the policy recommendation (e.g., Congress), and those stakeholders who will try to *influence* that decision (e.g., industry, citizens).

Having distinguished between decsionmakers and influencers, the researcher needs to ascertain the power of those stakeholders who will try to influence the policy decision. Power of a stakeholder is defined as follows by three dimensions (Doty, 1980; Dye, 1978; Etzioni, 1976):

- *amount* of resources available to the stakeholder;
- *ability* of stakeholder to mobilize resources; and
- *access* of stakeholder to decisionmakers.

Amount of resources refers to the wealth, political sophistication, and membership size (i.e., number of people represented by the stakeholder's organization) that the stakeholder can bring to bear to influence a policy decision. The type of resources that might be used include money, volunteers, contacts, information—all of which the decisionmakers may find helpful in proceeding with a particular study recommendation.

Ability to mobilize resources, a second dimension of power, refers to the extent of internal cohesion, consensus, and leadership that can be used to organize the members of a stakeholder's organization for action. Highly centralized groups with committed members led by a strong leader tend to be more influential than other stakeholders.

Finally, access to decisionmakers, the third dimension of power, is the extent to which the stakeholder is offered the opportunity to share information and opinions directly with the decisionmakers, without the interference of other individuals. Access is typically measurable by the number of gate-keepers between the decisionmakers and stakeholder, and the decisionmaker's receptivity and interest in meeting with the stakeholder. The more willing the decisionmakers are to listen to the stakeholders, the greater the stakeholder's potential for influencing any decisions that are made.

Together, these three dimensions will dictate the power of the stakeholder to influence the decisionmakers. In this way, a stakeholder can be analyzed as an important determinant of a study recommendation's implementability. An example of a powerful stakeholder is the group, Parents United for Full Public School Funding—an 800-member Washington, D.C., parents' group. This group has been cited as a powerful lobbying force pressuring the D.C. council to increase public school funds (Washington *Post,* 1983b). In an analysis of their successful lobbying efforts, the Washington *Post* explains their success as stemming from their effective use of their resources, strong leadership, and access to council members. Their activities have included distributing a fact sheet outlining consequences of budget cuts, meeting with City Council members to discuss the budget, mailings to local citizens providing names and telephone numbers of council members and dates of public hearings, and appearances on local television to rally support for their efforts. These activities have made them "an influential organization that [successfully] fought for a substantial budget increase in the current fiscal year" (Washington *Post,* 1983b, II p. B3).

Having determined the power of each stakeholder, the next step in the stakeholder analysis is to assess the opinion of each stakeholder about the study's policy recommendation. Will the stakeholder support or oppose the recommendation? Why? Regardless of the extent to which the stakeholder can influence the final decision, answers to these questions will provide valuable information on the level of support that the recommendation can be expected to generate.

Once the power and opinion of each stakeholder has been assessed, a picture of the power structure underlying the proposed recommendation can be constructed. A power structure is a description of the natures, strengths, and directions of the coalitions of stakeholders involved in the proposed recommendation. Specifically, the power structure provides a synthesis of information on the following four characteristics of the stakeholders:

(1) identification of key stakeholders;
(2) direction of stakeholders' support or opposition to the recommendation;
(3) power position of stakeholders relative to key decisionmakers; and
(4) probable support of key decisionmakers to implement recommendations, given the power and opinion of stakeholders.

One convenient way to visualize a power structure is with the use of vector diagrams. An example of a hypothetical vector diagram describing a simplified power structure is presented in Figure 5.1. In this diagram, members of congressional committees have been identified as the key decisionmakers, influenced in varying degrees by eight stakeholder groups. The influence or power of each group over the key decisionmakers is illustrated in the diagram by the relative distance between the stakeholder and decisionmakers: The closer the stakeholder to the decisionmakers, the greater the stakeholder's power. For the hypothetical example presented in the figure, the medical community is by far the most powerful group, followed by HHS (U.S. Department of Health and Human Services), and the Moral Majority.

Furthermore, in diagramming the power structure, the varying levels of support or opposition to the recommendation of each stakeholder group is indicated (i.e., by pluses and minuses in the figure). In the hypothetical example, opponents of the recommendation feel strongly about their opposition, while one of the four proponents (HHS) can give only lukewarm support.

By constructing the power structure that underlies a proposed recommendation, the researcher can begin to assess the likelihood that the recommendation will have sufficient political support to be adequately implemented. For the hypothethical example in Figure 5.1, opposition to the recommendation is sufficiently strong and the opposing stakeholders exert sufficient power over the decisionmakers that the decisionmakers probably would choose not to implement the recommendation.

If an initial assessment of the power structure indicates that the level of support may be insufficient for implementation (as was see in the hypothetical example), the researcher will want to begin considering ways in which either the stakeholders or the recommendation can be changed to enhance the level of political support (Seidl, 1978). Suggestions for making these changes are offered in the final section of this chapter.

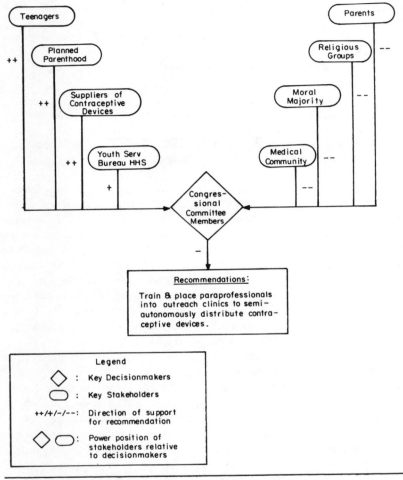

Figure 5.1 Hypothetical Power Structure of a Policy Recommendation

Analysis of Organizational Parameters

Analyzing the stakeholders involved in a particular policy recommendation is undoubtedly one important aspect of determining if a recommendation will be adequately implemented. By emphasizing power to the neglect of organization, however, one runs the risk of beginning a symbolic reform effort incapable of inducing lasting structural change (Doty, 1980). Therefore, organizational parameters affecting the likelihood that a recommendation will be adequately implemented should also be analyzed.

Conducting this analysis involves an evaluation of the three following organizational parameters:

(1) organizational structure for implementation,
(2) amount of resources needed for implementation, and
(3) policy mechanisms needed to encourage implementation.

Each of these parameters will be presented in different ways for different types of recommendations. A recommendation that involves allocating resources to schools may necessitate substantial resources, cooperation of local schools, and a hierarchical allocation system that functions fairly and efficiently. A recommendation that mandates minimum performance standards to schools, on the other hand, involves lower cash outlays, while necessitating a substantial organizational commitment to ensure compliance with the new standards. Despite the fact that recommendations will need different types of organizational parameters to be implemented, analysis of those parameters can be generally done in the same ways. Therefore, guidelines for conducting an analysis of organizational parameters are presented.

The first parameter—organizational structure—involves a structural description of the organization or organizations responsible for administering implementation of the recommendation. A description of the organization should include the type, size, and number of the organizations needing to be involved, as well as their hierarchical allocation of authority and control. For example, the organizational structure for implementing a recommendation concerning the now defunct Community Development Block Grant, legislation giving local communities funds to build fair housing, would involve the U.S. Department of Housing and Urban Development (HUD), state and regional agencies, city governments, and local community groups. In addition, for such a recommendation, there would be a fair amount of autonomy at lower levels in the hierarchy, such that what was implemented by local communities might differ from the intent at the HUD level. In the words of one administrator of a policy research center, "central agencies are often not aware that a recommended action might require considerable changes by the local agencies (Nagel & Neef, 1978, p. 17). Therefore, in analyzing a study recommendation, the type of organization as well as the degree of autonomy exercised down the chain of command are factors that will greatly influence the likelihood of recommendations being implemented as intended.

A second organizational parameter in analyzing the likelihood that a study recommendation will be implemented is the amount of resources needed for implementation. Such resources as finances, personnel, capital needs, and materials should be assessed. An assessment of those resources needed for implementation should then be compared with resources currently possessed by the organization or organizations responsible for implementation. For example, if implementation necessitates staff with more specialized technical skills than those currently employed by the responsible organization, adequate implementation of the recommendation will be seriously hampered.

A final organizational parameter to be analyzed in assessing the possible implementation of a study recommendation is the set of policy mechanisms needed to ensure adequate implementation. As discussed in Chapter 2, policies can involve a range of mechanisms to achieve their intended purposes. The mechanism may simply involve providing information, or encouraging research and development efforts by others. Such mechanisms demand little more from the targeted population than attention.

Policy mechanisms can also be much more demanding on the target population, such as regulatory measures and the allocation of financial incentives and disincentives to encourage desired behavior. In analyzing this parameter of the study recommendation, the extent to which the recommendation demands that people change must first be assessed. Then, the mechanisms that can be used to achieve this change should be analyzed for their acceptability and feasibility.

To illustrate the use of policy mechanisms, a recommendation to reduce a country's birth rate demands change among the population in their attitudes and behaviors about birth control. Efforts to achieve this change can involve a variety of different policy mechanisms. Such mechanisms could range from those that expect only voluntary contraceptive use, to those that coerce the use of birth control (e.g., compulsory sterilization, minimum marriage age, and tax penalties for excessive reproduction). In general, the more coercive the policy mechanism, the less acceptable it will be. However, some very coercive mechanisms (e.g., the 55 mph speed limit) have been successfully implemented in large segments of the population. Therefore, in assessing the likelihood that a particular recommendation will be implemented, the range of appropriate policy mechanisms should be analyzed for their feasibility in the current sociopolitical environment.

Having completed an analysis of the implementation parameters, you will have information pertaining to both the stakeholders and the organizational structures involved if the recommendation were to be implemented. This information will then be used in conjunction with another piece of information to estimate the probability that the recommendation, as it is currently conceived, will be sufficiently implemented to achieve the desired result. The other piece of information to be used in this estimation is an assessment of the potential consequences of the recommendation.

PREDICT POTENTIAL CONSEQUENCES OF RECOMMENDATIONS

An important determinant of the successful implementation of a study recommendation is the set of consequences caused by the implemented recommendation. Obviously, one cannot wait until the recommendation is actually implemented to identify those consequences. Therefore, the consequences must be predicted. Specifically, the following three types of predictions need to be made:

(1) possible intended and unintended effects of the recommendation;
(2) possible interactive effects of the recommendation on other policies and programs; and
(3) direction likely to be followed if the recommendation is not implemented.

In suggesting a particular course of action, a policy researcher does so with the intent that the suggestion will yield certain effects or consequences (e.g., reduced crime rate, fairer housing practices, and so on). In addition to the intended effects, however, the recommendation will probably have unintended effects as well. For example, the food stamp program was originally intended to provide the poor with the means to meet their nutritional requirements. However, in addition to serving the poor, food stamps were used by college students as a form of subsidy for college education—an unintended effect (Coates, 1978).

Another example of unintended effects can be found by examining federal antipoverty programs that were conceived to deal with issues such as adequate housing and job training (Horowitz & Katz, 1975). Since the programs tended to give localized minority groups new power, at the expense of groups with entrenched power, hostility between the groups tended to intensify rather than dissipate as a result of the programs. Labor was an issue of such hostility. "Minority group members can be trained to occupy skilled labor occupations. Yet unless other new job opportunities are created for white workers, there will only be replacement, not upward mobility. The white worker will then become an opponent of the newly-trained minority group" (Horowitz & Katz, 1975, p. 135). Unintended consequences, therefore, can become so prominent as to overshadow the original intent of the recommendation. In such situations, the probability that the recommendation will be adequately implemented is minimal.

A second type of prediction that needs to be made is the possible interactive effects of the recommendation on other policies and programs. Since policies are rarely independent of one another, the possible effects that a recommendation may have on other policies needs to be assessed. For example, a recommendation for the double indexing of social security taxes to both wages and prices would have more effects than simply altering social security payments to the elderly. Such a recommendation would also effect the financial stability of the social security trust fund, the consumption patterns of the elderly, and the spending of industries that belong to the social security system (Wildavsky, 1979). Clearly, a recommendation with potential effects on such a complex array of programs would necessitate a greater breadth of support than a recommendation having fewer interactive effects.

A final type of prediction that needs to be made is the direction likely to be followed by the social system if the recommendation is ignored (Kahn, 1969). The question of what is likely to happen to the social problem if the current policy efforts remain unchanged must be addressed. It may be the case that, without a new policy or intervention, the social problem will become less problematic on its own accord, making the implementation of a recommendation less necessary. On the other hand, there may be ample evidence to indicate that without a new policy, the social problem may have serious negative consequences in the foreseeable future. Such an ominous prediction can provide a powerful impetus to implement a proposed recommendation.

In making these three types of predictions, the policy researcher has a variety of tools and information sources available. Stakeholders can be informally interviewed (using "if . . . then" statements, for example) to assess the possibility of a range of consequences (Teune, 1978). Or the researcher may want to involve stakeholders in a more formal assessment process. One such procedure, called multiattribute utility modeling, involves a quantitative means for combining stakeholders' projections about future consequences (Snapper & Seaver, 1981).

Another formal method for making predictions is to involve subject matter experts in a Delphi procedure (Harman & Press, 1978; Moore [in press] in this series). A Delphi procedure involves obtaining initial predictions from individual experts. These predictions are shared among the experts, who are then asked to revise their predictions. This feedback and revision process continues until consensus among the experts has been achieved.

A final procedure for making predictions is a highly technical method called risk analysis (Kraft, 1982). Risk analysis is the process whereby "risks" associated with the recommendation are identified by the researchers; severity of harm is estimated, and acceptability of risk is determined. For example,

James Dyer (1982) describes a formula he developed to evaluate the risks (defined as the probability of death) associated with the presence of asbestos in building insulation material. Although risk analysis has great potential for the policy research process, risks associated with policy options may not be sufficiently understood as yet to be quantified (Fischer, 1980).

ESTIMATING THE PROBABILITY
OF IMPLEMENTATION

At this point in the policy research process, the researcher will have a general assessment of the stakeholders' power structure underlying the recommendation, the organizational structure involved in implementing the recommendation, and the potential consequences of the recommendation, if it is or is not implemented. With this information, the researcher is now ready to estimate a "subjective probability of implementation." The subjective probability is a statement of the chances, or odds, that a recommendation is feasible and acceptable enough to be implemented adequately. Note that this probability statement concerns only the probability of implementation; the probability or likelihood that the recommendation would be effective, if implemented properly, should have been answered before the recommendation was ever suggested (Simmons & Saunders, 1974).

The probability of implementation is subjective since it is based on information that is interpreted by the policy researcher. Formal procedures, however, can help to make the subjective nature of the probability estimate somewhat less biased. For example, regression models of a policy's political acceptability can be constructed (see Fischer, 1980), or Bayesian decision-analytic tools can be used to synthesize the information into one probability estimate (Bunn & Thomas, 1978). Formal procedures are not essential, however, particularly because the state of the art in making such probability estimates is not sufficiently advanced to warrant undue precision. Therefore, a "ballpark" estimate, such as a recommendation having a 20-40% chance of being implemented, is usually sufficient.

In addition to providing a measure to evaluate the feasibility of a specific recommendation, probability estimates serve two other functions. First of all, such estimates provide the means to compare *alternative* recommendations. As discussed earlier, a policy research study should pose several different courses of action for resolving a social problem. With these estimates, then, the policymaker will be able to determine which recommendation, relative to the other recommendations, has the greatest potential for implementation. Additionally, these subjective probability estimates also provide a built-in mechanism for gaining experience in implementation probabilities and factors affecting their success. Using probability estimates, policy researchers can assess over time how accurate their probability statements were, why they may have been inaccurate, and what corrections can be made in the future.

PREPARATION OF FINAL RECOMMENDATIONS

Having analyzed each study recommendation, you now have a set of subjective probabilities for each recommendation's being adequately implemented. The next step in the policy research process is to evaluate these implementation probabilities in light of the goals of the policy recommendations. Therefore, the following question must be answered: Is the probability sufficiently large to provide the recommendation with an opportunity to affect the social problem in the intended fashion? Although only you can answer this question, we suggest that probabilities lower than 60 percent necessitate a negative answer.

If you determine that the probability of implementation is sufficiently large, you can leave the initial recommendations as they are. However, if you do not feel that the probability is sufficiently large, the following three options are available.

(1) Accept the low implementation probability.
(2) Change the goals of the recommendations.
(3) Modify the recommendations.

First, as a policy researcher, you can always choose to leave your initial recommendations as they are, despite your feelings that they probably will not be adequately implemented. You may be accused by others of failing to meet your responsibility; nevertheless, you will not be the first or last researcher to select such an option.

Instead of simply accepting the low implementation probability, however, an alternative is to leave the recommendations essentially the same, while changing their goals. For example, a recommendation that may be initially focused on incremental change may actually be more implementable as a fundamental change (Boeckmann, 1976; Huitt, 1968). Although the New Jersey Income Maintenance Experiment initially intended to address incremental questions of an income maintenance program, public and congressional pressure forced it to take on the characteristics of a major welfare reform (Boeckmann, 1976). Goals need not always be changed from incremental to fundamental, or the converse. Goals may also change from a desire actually to implement the change to a desire to obtain agreement on change, if such a change were to be implemented (Wildavsky, 1979). Although a goal of consensus seems considerably more modest than a goal of actual change, it may be more realistic. Finally, goals may change from a focus on political activity to political education. "Political education is part of the legislative process, and a succession of defeats may be necessary to prepare the way for an ultimate victory that in retrospective seems inevitable" (Huitt, 1968, p. 264).

Instead of either changing the goals or accepting the low probability of implementation, the researcher may prefer the option of modifying the initial study recommendations to increase their implementation probabilities. We offer three ways of making such modification.

One way of modifying the recommendations to enhance their likelihood of implementation is to change the power structure of the stakeholders concerned with each recommendation. Strategies for altering the power structure can include strengthening the position of the stakeholders supporting the recommendation, weakening the position of the stakeholders opposed to the recommendation, or building a new coalition of supporters. The precise modifications made to the recommendations will depend on the strategy selected for altering the power structure, the type of power structure needed to obtain adequate support for the recommendation, and the areas of flexibility in the stakeholders' existing power structure. For example, a power structure involving inflexible opponents may necessitate a strategy that strengthens the power base of existing proponents. Or a power structure comprised of stakeholders in conflict over certain aspects of the recommendation may need to have the recommendation appeal to a new set of interests in order to create a new coalition of supporters.

In order to alter the existing power structure in accordance with your preferred strategy, you will need to present the proposed modification to the stakeholders and assess their reactions. It will probably be necessary to suggest alternative modifications to the recommendation to determine which one achieves the desired reaction. As individuals representing either themselves or a group, the stakeholders will react to different modifications in a way that may be difficult to predict precisely. With experience, however, the policy researcher can hope to gain a better feeling for the types of modifications that will work in different situations. Until that experience has accrued the four suggestions offered below will be helpful. These suggestions present ways of modifying recommendations for successfully altering the power structure that have worked for other policy researchers:

(1) Involve stakeholders in the modification process; this will help to create ownership and support for the new recommendation (Etzioni, 1976).
(2) Repackage the recommendation using terms and orientations appealing to stakeholders (Bergman, 1975).

(3) Emphasize in the recommendation the mutuality of interests between the desires of stakeholders and the public good (Bachrach, 1972).

(4) Redirect recommendations to provoke public controversy in an effort to deepen public concern and build strong support for meaningful actions (Bachrach, 1972).

As described above, one way to modify recommendations to enhance their likelihood of implementation is to change the recommendations specifically in an effort to alter the stakeholders' power structure. A second way of modifying the recommendations is to make the recommended actions more incremental in nature. Since such a modification affects not only the power structure, but the organizational parameters and potential consequences as well, this way of modifying recommendations is discussed separately from those mentioned above.

In general, the probability of implementation is higher among those recommendations that appear to be fairly incremental in nature than those that are more fundamental; that is, although a recommendation may stem from a perceived need to make fundamental changes in the social structure, the more the recommendation can be tied to existing policies, the less resistance the recommendation will face. For example, a recommendation to increase the female labor force may be tied to either a need to increase women's social equality or a need to increase the economic viability of the country by increasing the size of the skilled labor force. By tying the recommendation to issues of economic rather than social development, the recommendation will be less likely to incur the wrath of a patriarchal social structure. It should be noted that the goal of the recommendation is an increased female labor force whether or not it is tied to social or economic development. However, by tying the recommendation to one issue and not the other, the possibility of implementation is greatly enhanced.

In modifying recommendations to be more incremental, a continuum of incrementalism needs to be kept in mind. Recommendations can be made only to appear to be incremental such that the same goal is still achieved, as described in the example above; or recommendations can be modified to be so incremental as to be too weak to accomplish ostensible goals (Doty, 1980). Finally, recommendations can be modified to provide solutions that fall somewhere in the middle of the continuum. These solutions, called "halfway houses" (Huitt, 1968) provide only partial solutions to a social problem, such as a recommendation proposing housing subsidies to minority groups rather than a restructuring of the fair housing concept. Although such partial solutions hardly resolve the problem, they can provide steps in the right direction. When the choice is between a few small steps or no steps at all, the policy researcher may prefer to take the few steps.

A final suggestion for modifying recommendations to increase their likelihood of implementation is to alter the organizational structure for implementation. For example, if the organization responsible for implementation consists of fairly autonomous subordinate units (e.g., local communities), the recommendation should be rephrased to allow for a certain amount of "adaptive implementation" down the chain of command (Berman, 1980). Alternately, if the recommendation necessitates a fair amount of compliance by the targeted population, policy mechanisms appropriate for both the community and the level of compliance needed should be used (Etzioni, 1976). The policy mechanism may need to be unmitigated coercion, such as exists for the payment of federal taxes. A utilitarian mechanism that offers financial incentives and other ploys to motivate change may also be sufficient. Incentives to private industry for engaging in research and development is an example of such a mechanism. Finally, a mechanism that simply appeals to citizen's normative considerations may yield the level of compliance desired. For example, China's family planning program has been based on such normative compliance strategies as legitimizing family planning by the oft-quoted phrases of Mao Zedong (Stokes, 1977).

Apparent from these suggestions for modifying recommendations, this stage of the policy research process may pose some difficult dilemmas for the policy researcher. At what point do modifications become so extensive that the recommendations are no longer based on the technical analyses? Should the recommendations become more incremental with less potential for substantial change, or more fundamental with less potential for implementation? Should recommendations be restructured to gain the support of the stakeholders with whom you may fundamentally disagree? These are some of the questions that you, as a policy researcher, will need to face repeatedly over the course of your research. There are no "right" answers, and any answers that you propose will probably change over time. Therefore, as you continue to do policy research, you must accept the responsibility of struggling with these questions in the hope that one day you may achieve satisfaction with your answers.

EXERCISES

1. List questions you will need to address to the stakeholders involved in a particular policy recommendation to analyze adequately the implementation parameters involved in the recommendation.

2. List steps involved to analyze the study recommendations sufficiently to estimate their probability of implementation.

3. Suppose your old high school is considering an educational work experience program for the students. Further suppose that the high school principal appoints a committee of teachers to study the possibility of such a program, and the committee

turns to you to do a policy research study. As part of your study, you canvass for the opinions of stakeholders about potential advantages and disadvantages of the program. Based on your findings, you recommend the following:

A work experience program should be implemented as a *required* part of the high school curriculum.

Draw a diagram of the power structure underlying this recommendation. Who are the decisionmakers? Based on your power structure, will the recommendation be implemented? Why or why not?

4. "Last spring, Sen. Daniel Patrick Moynihan (D-NY) introduced a bill to require a simple accounting of which roads and bridges in the country were in the worst shape—so Congress could figure out how much pressing work had to be done and what it might cost. By the time this bill emerged from the warrens of the various subcommittees of the House Public Works and Government Operations Committees, it required not just a list of collapsing roads and bridges but an 'inventory and assessment' of all the nation's highways plus all firehalls, parks, landfills, garbage trucks, courthouses, pipelines, mass transit facilities, airports, power generating plants, playgrounds, sewers, and television stations" Washington *Post*, 1982). Why might a bill initially focused on roads and bridges be modified in such a fashion? Do you think that the bill was passed by Congress? If yes, why; if no, why not?

6

Communicating Policy Research to Policymakers

In this chapter four guidelines for productive communicative relationships between policy researchers and policymakers are presented.

In the preceding chapters, we have discussed the various steps involved in a policy research study: from preparation and conceptualization to technical analysis and recommendations analysis. A key component of the policy research process that has not yet been discussed at any length concerns the dynamics of communication between the policy researcher and the policymakers. Without an adequate communicative relationship between the researcher and policymakers, it will be exceedingly difficult for the researcher to ensure that research findings and recommendations are implemented. In fact, without open, active, and constructive communication between the policy researcher and policymaker, the policy research efforts will have little value.

Aside from increasing the likelihood that a policy research study will be used, close communicative relationships between policymakers and researchers offer several additional benefits as well. These benefits include the following:

- Teaching *policymakers* to appreciate constraints and realities of research to reduce the scepticism with which research is viewed.
- Teaching *policy researchers* about constraints and realities of the policymakers' world.
- Keeping *policymakers* knowledgeable about information that may be relevant at future times.
- Keeping *policy researchers* knowledgeable about changes in the policy arena that may affect the study.

Apparent from this short list of benefits is that close communication helps both policymakers and policy researchers. Without close communication, both parties may lose.

A communication process that is open, active, and productive does not happen serendipitously or without ample commitment by both parties. Unfortunately, until policymakers become convinced of the relevance and usefulness of social science research, the burden of developing a close, communicative relationship falls largely on the shoulders of the policy researcher. This burden tends to be particularly great when the study has not been specifically commissioned by a particular user, or the ownership of potential study users has not been adequately cultivated during the study. In such situations, the access to the policymakers may be very limited, making communication somewhat difficult.

Amitai Etzioni, a noted sociologist, describes an example of the difficulties involved in communicating policy recommendations (Etzioni, 1981). These difficulties arose when he was a senior advisor to the White House during the Carter administration. For two years, Etzioni tried unsuccessfully to interest the administration in the notion of a reindustrialization program which would restore America to "economic vigor." By his account, his lack of success was attributable to such circumstances as turf battles (economics was not perceived to be within the turf of a sociologist), an economically conservative administration, and an overuse of the notion of reindustrialization so that its true meaning was misunderstood and lost. Given these circumstances, Etzioni emerged from his experience with the following advice: "Outsiders who seek to promote policy ideas uninvited, especially without the backing by an organized societal group, lobby, or pressure group, will usually find the process tortuous. Those who choose to travel this road should understand that as a rule they are in for a long haul" (1981, p. 29).

It is apparent from Etzioni's experience that productive communicative relationships between researchers and policymakers may not be easily accomplished. To minimize the potential difficulties, this chapter discusses four major guidelines for communicating policy research to policymakers. By following these guidelines, we hope that the potential benefits associated with good communicative relationships can be achieved. These are the four guidelines:

- Communicate throughout the study.
- Communicate to different study users.
- Presentation may mean everything in effective communication.
- Oral communication is generally more effective than written.

GUIDELINE 1:
COMMUNICATE THROUGHOUT THE STUDY

Policy decisions tend to be made at any point, whether or not information is available. As a result, it is a rare situation that findings from a single, completed research study are disseminated at a time that precisely coincides with a critical decision point in the policymaking process (Coleman, 1975).

Due to this state of affairs, an extremely important guideline is that *communication with policymakers should start at the inception of the research study and continue actively throughout its duration.* In other words, to wait until the study has been completed before beginning communication and dissemination activities is seriously to hamper the likelihood that the study will be used.

An important aspect of communicating throughout a policy research study is that the communication should be two-way. Don't simply give the policymakers information; relay information so that feedback can be obtained. The researcher should consciously try to learn from the communication as well as to impart information. In this way, knowledge can be optimally used. In the words of Aaron Wildavsky, "To be knowledgeable is not necessarily to be wise" (1979, p. 402).

In communicating throughout the study, researchers should recognize that the policymaker is primarily interested in study results and recommendations. Design issues, data collection problems, and so forth are of less concern. Therefore, discussions with policymakers should always be related to results and recommendations—either with hints of what *will* be proposed or implications for what *can* be proposed (e.g., given the design constraints). By relating study progress to study outcome, researchers can also begin to test the feasibility of certain ideas they may be considering as possible recommendations. If the policymakers express strong opposition to the ideas, alternate recommendations may need to be considered. By discussing these ideas with the policymakers prior to delivering a formal proposal, the researcher also provides the policymakers needed time to absorb and adjust to the new ideas. Many policymakers tend initially to respond quite negatively to innovative ideas; with additional time for unpressured reflection, however, their reactions may become more supportive.

In communicating with policymakers, policy researchers should not limit themselves to direct discussions with the policymakers. Daniel Koretz (1982) suggests using several other communication channels to relay information and obtain feedback. These channels include the personal staff of policymakers, news media, and interest groups with access to the policymakers. By "extending the number of points of access" (Fraatz, 1982, p. 276), and sharing information through these alternate routes, policymakers may hear as much, if not more than through direct conversation.

To suggest that communication should start early and continue throughout the study does not deemphasize the importance of timing in presenting final results. In fact, based on years of doing policy research about children, Eleanor Maccoby and her colleagues discuss what they feel is perhaps the most important lesson to learn: "Know the right times and places for introducing your information to the policymaking process" (1983, p. 80). They describe an example of a report, "Policies for Children," that was produced at the right time. The report was able to answer a decade-old question about the effects of different teacher-child ratios in day care facilities. By answering this question, a major bridge to establishing federal standards for day care was finally crossed.

Although the "right" time and "right" place clearly depend on the policy issue under study, one piece of advice has been offered by Brim and Dustan:

> If a senator sits on a committee with jurisdiction over a bill, the time to approach that person is *before* the committee has reported on the bill. Similarly, a legislator usually seeks quite specific information, not general background on the bill. (1983, p. 85)

With this advice, and the advice of others, proceed throughout the policy research effort always with an eye to the right place and time.

To communicate throughout a study does not imply that results should be disseminated prior to completion of the technical analysis. Rather, information communicated at any time should only be that which is either strongly supportable or understood to be an opinion. Unfortunately, as simple as this rule seems, policy researchers may occasionally find themselves pressured to release findings before the technical analysis is completed.

Margaret Boeckmann (1976) describes a situation in which midway through a research experiment on guaranteed annual income, pertinent legislation was introduced to Congress. Given the introduction of the legislation, the researchers responsible for the experiment were in the unfortunate position of either providing Congress with very preliminary and potentially incorrect results, or not responding to Congress when the need was greatest. The researchers chose the former option and presented their results. Unfortunately, the preliminary results were greeted with such harsh scepticism about their credibility that when the study was completed it was ignored. Hindsight, then, would suggest that the researchers made the wrong decision. However, if the researchers had remained mute, accusations about the irrelevance of social science research would have abounded. The solution for the researchers was not a simple one. If you find yourself in a similar situation, the trade-offs between silence and relevance must be weighed carefully.

GUIDELINE 2:
COMMUNICATE TO DIFFERENT USERS

As discussed in earlier chapters, policy research studies tend to have several different users with a variety of interests. To ensure that a policy research study is adequately disseminated, then, the policy researcher should communicate the study differently to the different users. Some users will desire more detailed information, some will only want the major findings, and some will only want information that directly helps them. For example, in a study of projects to encourage parental involvement, study users included both Congress and local project directors (Smith & Robbins, 1982). While "Congress" was interested in an overview of the major findings, local project directors were only interested in recommendations about techniques for increasing parental involvement. Obviously, no one, single approach to communicating the results to both parties would have adequately served their different needs.

Because the policy researcher must be able to involve different users successfully in the communication process, a policy researcher needs to have a kind of "psychic profile" enabling "effective interaction with politicians, bureaucrats, housewives, and minority leaders" (Etzioni, 1971, p. 10). Such a "profile" involves, at the minimum, three abilities. These abilities include (1) translating research nomenclature and procedures into concepts understandable to the different audiences, (2) recognizing when detail should be explained, and (3) structuring communication so that the audience does not feel intellectually inferior. These abilities are not taught in college as students usually interact with other students of comparable intelligence and knowledge. Therefore, an inexperienced policy researcher will need to be particularly aware of this guideline if the policy research study is to be effectively communicated to the decisionmakers. Remember: Individuals who are made to feel inferior because they do not understand "beta coefficients" will not be favorably inclined toward the study recommendations.

One caution is needed in recognizing that communication involves a variety of users. It is possible that in the communication process too many users may be involved. For example, in a study of the Cities-In-Schools project (Stake, 1983), the "stakeholders were diverse and far-flung," including federal and private funders, political and evangelical solicitations (Jesse Jackson), and beneficiaries in each of the nation's large cities. An "attempt to be useful to many, [including this many stakeholders as users] may have prevented the report from being useful to any" (Stake, 1983, p. 25). Therefore, while addressed to a diverse audience, a report should not become so fragmented as to be useless.

GUIDELINE 3:
EFFECTIVE PRESENTATION CREATES THE BASIS
FOR GOOD COMMUNICATION

A researcher can begin communicating with study users early on in the research process and continue throughout. The researcher can also gear any communication to precisely the appropriate level and interest of each study user. Despite these efforts, however, the policy research study will not be effectively communicated and used if the study is not presented properly. Therefore, a third important guideline to remember is that *effective presentations form the basis for determining the ultimate utility of the policy research study.*

Ellen Greenberger, a researcher concerned with the adolescent work force, described testimony she gave at a hearing on proposed regulatory changes designed to increase work opportunities among adolescents (1983). In preparation for her testimony, she asked the staff of the House

TABLE 6.1
Advice for Effective Presentations
at a Congressional Hearing

Should the testimony be written? The answer (unhappily, given the shortness of time, but predictably) was "yes"—and bring 75 copies with you for distribution to media persons. Heavy coverage by the press and television networks is expected.

Should I read it or ad lib it? Since you're an academic, you're probably a better writer than most people (sic). Read it.

How long should I plan to speak? About 10-20 minutes.

How much detail about the methods and design or our research should be given? Virtually none. People can ask you afterwards or consult your papers. Bring copies of all your papers that are relevant to the testimony.

Can I draw on research other than our own? I think it would strengthen the case. Sure.

Can I express opinions, or must I only present data? You can express opinions. And when you present data, emphasize your conclusions.

Are strong words okay? Yes, within reasonable limits.

Which interests are behind the proposed changes in regulations? Most people think the restaurant and amusement park industries are the moving forces.

Who else will be testifying, and what are they likely to say? A spokesperson for the Labor Department, speaking in favor of the proposed changes, of course; the Secretary-Treasurer of the AFL-CIO, against, on the grounds that increasing the supply of subminimum wage labor will take jobs away from older youth and adults, and exploit young workers. . . . (This information helped me to anticipate the other testimony and suggested which topics that I might have mentioned would be better dealt with by others, and which topics, on the other hand, might benefit from repetition and from my drawing on a different line of evidence.)

SOURCE: Adapted from Greenberger (1983, pp. 105-106).

Subcommittee on Labor Standards for advice on her presentation. Her questions and answers are shown in Table 6.1. In addition to the questions, she offers the following observations for ensuring an effective presentation:

- Provide a summary at the beginning of both the written and spoken statements in order to show my colors clearly and quickly.
- Write throughout with some attention to "quotables" (e.g., "the proposed regulatory changes are a threat to young people's development . . .").
- Concentrate on research findings that are clearly linked to concerns with which the President's administration is closely identified.
- Phrase findings in terms of high visibility and impact. (1983, p. 107)

As a result of her effective presentation and those of others during the hearing, the proposed regulation was speedily withdrawn.

As illustrated in Ellen Greenberger's example, effective presentations are determined by two key elements: (1) the structure used to explain the study and (2) characteristics of the researcher or researchers presenting the study information. The structure refers to the oral or written style, format, and media used to explain a study to a user. Several suggestions for developing a structure which effectively communicates a study are offered.

First, in all presentations, a multimedia, multimethod approach to presentations is far more effective than the use of any single media or method (Brown & Braskamp, 1980). Multimedia refers to the use of slides, charts, briefing packets, or other visual or auditory aides that help to make a point. David Stockman, the director of the Office of Management and Budget for the Reagan administration, told the Washington *Post* (1983a) that he uses a very specific structure for presenting the difficulties of achieving a balanced budget to President Reagan. Stockman's structure involves a series of charts and graphs portraying projected trends in budget deficits. These charts are coupled with a "sobering multiple choice decision paper" on the budget. The decision paper actively involves Reagan in the presentation by having him check one of three boxes for each of 50 programs, indicating the level of spending Reagan prefers. Not surprisingly, the decision paper is structured such that, even if the lowest spending level is chosen for each program, a balanced budget cannot be achieved. By using this structure for presenting information, Stockman is able to achieve his objective of convincing Reagan that a balanced budget is not possible in the forseeable future. Also, by using this presentation, it is clear that "Stockman has figured out how Reagan works; and how to influence his decisions" (Washington *Post,* 1983, p. A1).

Aside from using multiple media, the researcher should also use multiple methods to explain a policy research study. Multiple methods might consist of detailed reports coupled with brief, two-page information sheets or oral briefings accompanied by written supporting documents. The Office of Technology Assessment, for example, uses three methods for communicating any study to Congress: a well-documented lengthy report involving appendices, a twenty-page pamphlet, and a one-page information sheet (Gibbons, 1983). The contents of each method are carefully reviewed to ensure that study methods, results, and recommendations are communicated consistently throughout.

In addition to using multiple media and methods, effective presentations of policy research studies should be simple and focused, consisting of only a few key points linked to specific issues and decisions (Brown & Braskamp, 1980). James Coleman (1975) describes a case in which policy researchers (Coleman included) predicted the results of a national election for the New York *Times* using a new forecasting method. Although the researchers completed the forecasting within ample time for election night reporting, the forecasts were not used, because, according to Coleman, the New York *Times* was presented with forecasts that were too complicated to be quickly understood.

As described in the foregoing paragraphs, an effective structure for presenting policy research studies consists of a few specially selected key points discussed using multiple media and multiple methods. Supplementing this general principle, several authors have made additional suggestions for further enhancing the structural effectiveness of presentations (Koretz, 1982; Smith & Robbins, 1982). These suggestions are briefly summarized below:

- Be concrete; use examples and anecdotes to make points more understandable.
- For each presentation, establish objectives to be accomplished during the presentation for both the audience and presenter.
- Conclusions and major caveats of the study should be presented first.
- The relationship of the study to policy questions should be explained.
- Avoid jargon—for example, change "study has little external validity" to "study's results cannot be generalized to the entire population."
- Discuss the differential effectiveness of relative options rather than the effectiveness of a single option.
- Clearly state study limitations about the selection of variables and generalizability of results.
- Reduce presentation to its essentials by justifying inclusion of any and all material.

These suggestions apply to both oral and written presentations.

In addition, written reports can be enhanced by following these three suggestions:

- Major points in each section of the report should be summarized at the beginning of each section.
- Headings for each section of the report should be used to encapsulate or convey information; for example, a heading such a "Few Parents Attended PTA" should be used rather than "Parent Attendance Patterns."
- Precede the body of the report with a summary of less than five single-spaced pages; the summary should be the most carefully written part of the report as it may be the only part read.

Together, these suggestions and principles constitute a very different type of presentation than that usually used in traditional research. Manuscripts styled after academic journal articles will not be read, much less understood. Furthermore, while creativity is not encouraged in the presentation of traditional research studies, creativity may make the difference in whether a policy research study is used. Therefore, be inventive! Use colors, pamphlets, pictures, or whatever may make the presentation more interesting to read or hear.

The suggestions discussed above have been offered to help create an effective structure for presenting policy research studies. An effective structure, alone, however, will not always be sufficient for effectively communicating the study to potential users.

In some situations, the effectiveness of a presentation may also be affected by the characteristics of the researchers who are conducting and presenting the study. The researcher's job title, gender, organizational affiliation, and so on, may all influence the extent to which a potential user readily accepts and uses the study. For example, in research conducted by Caplan in 1974 (cited in Horowitz & Katz, 1975), half of the policymakers surveyed indicated that it was necessary to be familiar with the social scientist in order to evaluate a set of findings. Apparently, then, characteristics such as the personal presence and "likability" of the researcher may help determine if a study will be used.

Given the occasional importance assigned to researcher characteristics, you may want to consider those characteristics in communicating policy research to potential users. For example, a member of a research team who has already developed a relationship with a potential user may be the best person to present the study—-even if that person was not the principal investigator.

Obviously, you should not allow researcher characteristics totally to direct the course of the presentation; however, you should be aware of their role.

The guideline discussed here—effective presentations as the basis for good communication—is directed at a key concept underlying the use of study results. That concept is credibility; the more credible the researcher and study are perceived to be, the more likely the study will be used (Boeckmann, 1976; Murphy, 1980). For example, read the following dialogue of a senator's legislative aide concerning why a particular experiment was not used:

> I guess that . . . there had been some discrediting of the experiment. That the size of the sample was small. That they had reported findings too early. I remember that when I had suggested to the senator that we use it in a statement to support our idea, he said no let's not emphasize that experiment because of its controversial nature. And I know that the Finance Committee had been attacking it. And whenever you are using data to support your position, you always try to come up with the strongest data possible, and if that information has already been attacked fairly strongly you decide well, we will drop that and go on to something that we have a great deal of confidence in. (cited in Boeckmann, 1976, p. 67)

For this experiment, circumstances had undermined its credibility and ruined its usability. In developing a presentation that effectively communicates your policy research study, then, try and anticipate those areas where credibility may be challenged (e.g., Have experts known to the policymakers been consulted? Were alternative interpretations of the data considered? Can study results be interpreted in light of the researchers' own stakes in the study?). By anticipating these questions and challenges before they are posed, you may be able to convince the policymakers that you have conducted a credible study worthy of their interest and use.

GUIDELINE 4:
ORAL COMMUNICATION IS USUALLY MORE EFFECTIVE THAN WRITTEN

Traditional research relies almost exclusively on the use of written materials (e.g., journal articles) to disseminate research findings. Even presentations at professional conferences are usually read from papers prepared in advance of the conference. In policy research, it is usually the spoken, rather than the written work, which is one of the most effective media for communication. This is particularly true when oral communication is coupled with a handout briefly describing key points. In the words of Jo Fraatz, "research is received more enthusiastically if disseminated by people rather than papers" (1982, p. 275).

Oral presentations of information tend to be effective for a variety of reasons. Policymakers are generally very busy people who do not have the time or motivation to read lengthy documents. By presenting the information verbally, in a concise format, policymakers can grasp the new information as quickly as possible. In addition, oral presentations allow policymakers to ask questions on the spot to enhance their understanding of the research findings. Finally, since an essential skill of a good policymaker is the effective use of speeches and oral arguments, policymakers typically feel much more comfortable and less defensive in settings which utilize their verbal rather than reading talents.

Given the effectiveness of oral communication, then, policy researchers should strive to enhance their verbal, as well as analytic skills. To think quickly "on your feet," to use both nonverbal and verbal cues, to "read" the audience, to anticipate questions and reactions, and to speak extemporaneously without notes are skills that warrant practice and preparation. Despite the effort involved in such preparation, however, the additional respect and credibility afforded you and your study will make it all worthwhile.

CLOSING

In this chapter, the importance of a close communicative relationship between the policy researcher and policymakers was discussed. Numerous specific guidelines for achieving this type of relationship were presented. Throughout these discussions, it was assumed that you, the policy researcher, would be the person responsible for communication—just as you are responsible for the preparation, conceptualization, technical analysis, and recommendations analysis. By having one central figure responsible for each phase of the policy research effort, information obtained in one phase can be used strategically in later phases.

Although a policy research effort requires the policy researcher to be responsible for all phases of the effort, the demands of doing each phase in an accurate and commendable fashion are overwhelming. Therefore, be prepared for initial failures; later successes will come. Perhaps the best advice to be offered at this point is to echo the words of one director of a policy research center: "Be tenacious!" One day your ship will come in.

EXERCISES

1. It has been argued that a researcher conducting a study should not be involved in advocating the study results, because by doing so, the researcher is no longer an objective, dispassionate scientist. Comment on this argument. Where would you draw the line between credible research and unadulterated advocacy?

2. Suppose that you planned to do a study for your college president about future educational needs of today's college-bound high school students. Find out enough about your president to plan out how you would communicate with him or her throughout the study and present the final results and recommendations. Discuss and describe your plan.

3. In a recent article in the Washington *Post* (1983c), a Pentagon briefer of Soviet weaponry is highlighted. The briefer, John T. Hughes, is a photo-intelligence analyst who has constructed a briefing that has been called "dramatic" and "brilliant." Standing behind a podium with pointer in hand, an assistant flashing one photograph after the next, Hughes runs down all the clues that indicate a monumental Soviet defense buildup. "His style is the dramatic understatement—straightforward, no obvious hyperbole, just the facts (some of the facts anyway), the overwhelming array, the panoramic display, the gruesome picture of a monstrous military powerhouse" (1983b, p. C2). Although Hughes's briefing is applauded by some, it is criticized by others as biased and incomplete. It does not compare the United States to the Soviet Union; it also tends to focus on only those facts which are alarming (i.e., the photographs that "look pretty damn scary"). Obviously, Hughes is very effective in supporting a particular position (the need to build up American military defenses). First, describe the structural features of the presentation that make him so effective. Then, discuss the ethical issues that Hughes's briefing presents (e.g., selective presentation of facts, no effort to caveat photographs, and so forth).

POLICY RESEARCH GLOSSARY

Numerals in parentheses refer to chapter numbers in which term was defined.

Basic social research: traditional academic research done on fundamental social problems; action orientation of research is low (1).

Champion: powerful decisionmaker willing to support a study and ensure that study results are appropriately utilized (2).

Client: user of the policy research study who either initiated the study, serves as a *funding source* for the study, and/or is interested in study results (2).

Cost benefit analysis: set of methods by which the costs and benefits to society of alternative policy options are compared (4).

Delphi procedure: method for obtaining a composite set of predictions about future events from subject matter experts (5).

Empirico-inductive: an adjective describing a research process where concepts and causal theories are induced from the empirical dynamic study of the social phenomenon; contrasts with *hypothetico-deductive* (1).

Enlightenment: term used by Weiss (1977) to describe the use of policy research for problem definition rather than problem resolution purposes (1).

Focused synthesis: a policy research method involving the selective review and integration of information relevant to particular research questions (4).

Fundamental change: change that offers new perspectives, assumptions, and goals (2).

Funding source: for policy research, the funding source may be a government agency, interest or constituency group, or a private philanthropic organization (1).

Hypothetico-deductive: an adjective describing a research process where social phenomenon are studied via specific predetermined hypotheses; contrasts with *empirico-inductive* (1).

Incremental change: change that focuses on fairly minor, short-term solutions within a framework of existing goals and assumptions (2).

Malleable variables: variables that are vulnerable to change, given the existing *sociopolitical environment* surrounding the social problem (3).

Mixed scanning change: a term used by Etzioni (1976) to describe changes which involve the formulation of fundamental new guidelines that are incrementally modified over time (2).

Operationalization: process whereby variables and concepts are defined in terms of measurable indicators (4).

Policy analysis: research done by political scientists interested in the process by which policies are adopted and the effects of the policies once adopted (1).

Policy mechanisms: tools or vehicles used by policymakers to achieve policy objectives (2).

Policymaking context: policy issues, decisionmaking process, stakeholders, and power structure involved in the policymaking environment surrounding a social problem (2).

Policy research: process of conducting research or analysis on a fundamental social problem in order to provide policymakers with pragmatic, action-oriented recommendations for alleviating the problem (1).

Politically significant findings: findings of a policy research study that warrant policy action (4).

Proxy indicators: indicators that reasonably substitute for a concept or variable that is difficult to measure directly (4).

Sociopolitical environment: the aspects of a social problem's context that include both sociological and political factors (2).

Stakeholders: individuals or groups who either have some input into decisionmaking about a social problem, or are affected by policy decisions on that problem (2).

Stakeholder power structure: description of the nature, strength and directions of the coalitions of stakeholders involved in a proposed recommendation (5).

Subjective probability of implementation: a statement of the chances, or odds, that a recommendation for policy action is feasible and acceptable enough to be adequately implemented (5).

Technical analysis: activities by which factors that may cause a social problem are studied (4).

Technical social research: research structured to resolve very specific, narrowly defined problems; action orientation is high (1).

REFERENCES

Aaron, H. J. (1978). *Politics and the professors*. Washington, DC: The Brookings Institution.

American Psychological Association (1982). Seat belts: Behavioral research is joined with efforts to shape policy. *American Psychological Association Monitor, 13*(12), 12-13.

Angell, R. (1965). *Free society and moral crisis*. Ann Arbor: University of Michigan Press.

Babbie, E. R. (1973). *Survey research methods*. Belmont, CA: Wadsworth.

Bachrach, P. (1972). The scholar and political strategy: The population case. In R. L. Clinton et al. (Eds.), *Political science in population studies*. Lexington, MA: Lexington Books.

Berelson, B. (1976). Social science research on population: A review. *Population and Development Review, 2*(2), 219-266.

Bergman, E. (1975). The political analysis of population policy choices. In R. Godwin (Ed.), *Comparative policy and analysis*. Lexington, MA: Lexington Books.

Berman, P. (1980). Thinking about programmed and adaptive implementation: Matching strategies to situations. In H. M. Ingram & D. E. Mann (Eds.), *Why policies succeed or fail*. Beverly Hills, CA: Sage.

Boeckmann, M. (1976). Policy impacts of the New Jersey Income Maintenance experiment. *Policy Sciences, 7*, 53-76.

Brandl, J. E. (1980). Policy evaluation and the work of legislature. In *New directions for program evaluators* (No. 5). San Francisco: Jossey-Bass.

Brim, O. G., & Dustan, J. (1983). Translating research into policy for children. *American Psychologist, 38* (1), 85-90.

Brown, R. D., & Braskamp, L. A. (1980). Summary: Common themes and a checklist. In *New directions for program evaluation* (No. 5). San Francisco: Jossey-Bass.

Brown, S. D. (1982). A case study of evaluation research in the legislature process: Public transportation for the handicapped. In *New directions for program evaluation* (No. 14). San Francisco: Jossey-Bass.

Bunn, K. W., & Thomas, H. (Eds.). (1978). *Formal methods in policy formulation*. Basel, Stuttgart: Birkhauser.

Burton, I. (1979, April). Policy directions for rural water supply in developing countries. *AID Program Evaluation Discussion Paper No.4*.

Cain, M., Khanam, S. R., & Nahar, S. (1979). Class, patriarchy, and the structure of women's work in rural Bangladesh. Center for Policy Studies, *Population Council Working Paper No. 43*.

Calder, B. J. (1977, August). Focus groups and the nature of qualitative marketing research. *Journal of Marketing Research*.

Campbell, D. T. (1969). Reforms as experiments. *American Psychologist, 24*, 409-429.

Caputo, D. A., & Cole, R. L. (1975). The initial impact of revenue sharing on the spending patterns of American cities. In K. M. Dolbeare (Ed.), *Public policy evaluation*. Beverly Hills, CA: Sage.

Carter, R. K., & Kosinski, R. D. (1981, Spring). Doing research in a politically charged environment. *New England Journal of Human Services*.

Cicirelli, V. G. et al. (1969, June). *The impact of Head Start: An evaluation of the effects of Head Start on children's cognitive and affective development.* Westinghouse Learning Corporation and Ohio University.

Coates, J. F. (1978). What is a public policy issue? In K. R. Hammond (Ed.), *Judgment and decision in public policy formation.* Boulder, CO: Westview.

Coleman, J. S. (1975). Problems of conceptualization and measurement in studying policy impacts. In K. M. Dolbeare (Ed.), *Public policy evaluation.* Beverly Hills, CA: Sage.

Commission on Population Growth and the American Future. (1972). *Population and the American future.* Final report.

Dexter, L. A. (1970). The job of the congressman. In I. Sharkansky (Ed.), *Policy analysis in political science.* Chicago: Markham.

Doty, P. (1980). *Guided change of the American health system: Where the levers are.* New York: Human Sciences Press.

Doty, P. (1982). The role of the evaluation research broker. In L. Saxe & D. Kroetz (Eds.), *New directions for program evaluation* (No. 14). San Francisco: Jossey-Bass.

Dror, Y. (1968). *Public policy making.* San Francisco: Chandler.

Dror, Y. (1971). Applied social science and system analysis. In I. L. Horowitz (Ed.), *The use and abuse of social science.* New Brunswick, NJ: E. P. Dutton.

Dye, T. R. (1978). *Understanding public policy* (3rd ed.). Englewood Cliffs, NJ: Prentice-Hall.

Dyer, J. S. (1982). An asbestos hazard index for managing friable asbestos insulating material. *Policy Studies Review, 1*(4), 656-665.

Edwards, J. (in press). *Self-report instruments.* Beverly Hills, CA: Sage.

Edwards, W., Guttentag, M., & Snapper, K. J. (1975). Effective evaluation: A decision-theoretic approach. In E. L. Streuning & M. Guttentag (Eds.), *Handbook of evaluation research.* Beverly Hills, CA: Sage.

Etzioni, A. (1971). Policy research. *The American Sociologist, 6,* 8-12.

Etzioni, A. (1976). *Social problems.* Englewood Cliffs, NJ: Prentice-Hall.

Etzioni, A. (1979). Beyond integration, toward equitability. In P. M. Hauser, *World population and development.* Syracuse, NY: Syracuse University Press.

Etzioni, A. (1982). Riding a whirlwind. *Society, 19*(3), 29-35.

Finsterbusch, K., & Motz, A. B. (1980). *Social research for policy decisions.* Belmont, CA: Wadsworth.

Fischer, F. (1980). *Politics, values, and public policy: The problem of methodology.* Boulder, CO: Westview.

Fowler, F. (1984). *Survey research methods.* Beverly Hills, CA: Sage.

Fraatz, J. M. (1983). Policy analysts as advocates. *Journal of Policy Analysis and Management, 1*(2), 273-276.

Gibbons, J. (1983). *Technology and federal policy: Confession of a wayward physicist.* Invited Address at the Washington, D.C., MIT Luncheon Club, January 20.

Ginsburg, L. H. (1982). Changing public attitudes about public welfare clients and services through research. *Policy Studies Journal, 10*(3), 581-590.

Glaser, B. G., & Strauss, A. L. (1967). *The discovery of grounded theory.* Chicago: Aldine.

Gorshick, L. B., & Williamson, J. B. (1982). The politics of measuring poverty among the elderly. *Policy Studies Journal, 10*(3), 483-498.

Greenberger, E. (1983). A researcher in the policy arena. *American Psychologist, 38*(1), 104-111.

Grob, G. N. (1981). Public policymaking and social policy. In I. Horowitz (Ed.), *Policy studies review annual* (Vol. 5). Beverly Hills, CA: Sage.

Guzzo, R. A., & Bondy, J. S. (1983). Assessing technological advancement using groups of experts. In K. Bunn & H. Thomas (Eds.), *Formal methods in policy formulation.* Basel, Stuttgart: Birkhauser.

Herriott, R. E. (1982). Tension in research design and implementation: The Rural Experiment Schools Study. *American Behavioral Scientist, 26*(1), 23-44.

Horowitz, I. L. (Ed.). (1971). *The use and abuse of social science.* New Brunswick, NJ: E. P. Dutton.

Horowitz, I. L., & Katz, J. E. (1975). *Social science and public policy in the United States.* New York: Praeger.

House, P., & Coleman, J. (1980). Realities of public policy analysis. In S. S. Nagel (Ed.), *Improving policy analysis.* Beverly Hills, CA: Sage.

Huitt, R. K. (1968). Political feasibility. In A. Ranney (Ed.), *Political science and public policy.* Chicago: Markham.

Ingram, H. M., & Mann, D. E. (1980). *Why policies succeed and fail.* Beverly Hills, CA: Sage.

Jones, C. O. (1970). *An introduction to the study of public policy.* Belmont, CA: Wadsworth.

Kahn, A. J. (1969). *Theory and practice of social planning.* New York: Russell Sage Foundation.

Koretz, D. (1982). Developing useful evaluation: A case history and some practical guidelines. *New directions for program evaluation* (No. 14). San Francisco: Jossey-Bass.

Kraft, M. E. (1982). The use of risk analysis in federal regulatory agencies: An exploration. *Policy Studies Review, 1*(4), 666-675.

Lamm, R. D. (1978). The environment and public policy. In K. R. Hammond (Ed.), *Judgment and decision in public policy formation.* Boulder, CO: Westview.

Lasswell, H. (1958). *Politics: Who gets what, when, how?* Cleveland: World.

Levin, H. M. (1979). Cost-effectiveness analysis in evaluation research. In M. Guttentag & E. L. Streuning (Eds.), *Handbook of evaluation research.* Beverly Hills, CA: Sage.

Lindblom, C. E., & Cohen, D. (1979). *Usable knowledge: Social science and social problem solving.* New Haven, CT: Yale University Press.

Louis, K. S. (1982). Multisite/multimethod studies, *American Behavioral Scientist, 26*(1), 6-22.

Lowi, T. (1964). American business, public policy, case studies, and political theory. *World Politics, 16,*(July), 677-715.

Lynd, R. S. (1939). *Knowledge for what?* Princeton, NJ: Princeton University Press.

Maccoby, E. E., Kahn, A. J., & Everett, B. A. (1963). The role of psychological research in the formation of policies affecting children. *American Psychologist, 38*(1), 80-84.

McCrae, D. (1980). Policy analysis methods and government functions. In S. Nagel (Ed.), *Improving policy analysis.* Beverly Hills, CA: Sage.

Maggiotto, M. A., & Bowman, A. (1982). Policy orientations and environmental regulation: A case study of Florida's legislators. *Environment & Behavior, 14*(2), 155-170.

Majchrzak, A., Schroeder, A., & Patchen, R. (1982). *State criteria and mechanisms for assessing the effectiveness and efficiency of social service block grant programs: Final report.* Rockville, MD: Westat. (DHHS Contract HEW-100-31-003)

Majone, G. (1980). Policies as theories. *Omega: The International Journal of Management Science, 8*(2).

Meehan, E. J. (1971). *The foundations of political analysis.* Homewood, IL: Dorsey.

Meltsner, A. (1976). *Policy analysts in the bureaucracy.* Berkeley: University of California Press.

Moore, C. (in press). *Group decision-making techniques.* Beverly Hills, CA: Sage.

Nagel, S. (1975). Choosing among alternative public policies. In K. M. Dolbeare (Ed.), *Public policy evaluation*. Beverly Hills, CA: Sage.

Nagel, S. (Ed.). (1980). *Improving policy analysis*. Beverly Hills, CA: Sage.

Nagel, S. (1982). Policy studies organization and policy studies developments. *Policy Studies Journal, 10*(3), 432-441.

Nagel, S. (1983). *Factors facilitating the utilization of legal policy evaluation research*. Unpublished paper.

Nagel, S., & Neef, M. (Eds.). (1978). *Policy research centers directory*. Urbana, IL: Policy Studies Organization.

Neiman, M., & Lovell, C. (1981). Mandating as a policy issue—the definitional problem. *Policy Studies Journal, 9*(5), 667-681.

Patton, M. Q. (1980). *Qualitative evaluation methods*. Beverly Hills, CA: Sage.

Planned Parenthood. (1977). *Planned births, the future of the family and the quality of American life*. New York: The Alan Guttmacher Institute.

Rein, M., & White, S. H. (1977). Can policy research help policy? *The Public Interest, 49*, 119-136.

Reutlinger, S., & Selowsky, M. (1976). *Malnutrition and poverty: Magnitude and policy options*. World Bank Staff Occasional Papers No. 23. Washington, DC: World Bank.

Rist, R. C. (1982). Beyond the quantitative cul-de-sac: A qualitative perspective on youth employment programs. *Policy Studies Journal, 10*(3), 522-538.

Robey, J. S. (1982). Major contributors to public policy analysis. *Policy Studies Journal, 10*(3), 442-447.

Rosenthal, R. (1984). *Meta-analysis*. Beverly Hills, CA: Sage.

Rossi, P. H., & Shlay, A. B. (1982). Residential mobility and public policy issues: "Why families move" revisited. *Journal of Social Issues, 38*(3), 21-34.

Rossi, P. H., Wright, J. D., & Wright, S. R. (1978). The theory and practice of applied social research. *Evaluation Quarterly, 2*(2), 171-191.

Salisbury, R. H., & Heinz, J. P. (1968). *A theory of policy analysis and some preliminary applications*. Paper presented at the American Political Association Convention, Washington, DC, September.

Saunders, L. (1972). Action needs: The relevance of political research. In R. L. Clinton et al. (Eds.), *Political science in population studies*. Lexington, MA: Lexington Books.

Schmidt, R. (1982). *Short-term policy-oriented research and evaluation: Opportunities and dilemmas*. Symposium at the American Psychological Association Convention, Washington, DC, August.

Seidl, J. M. (1976, September). *Development of a conceptual framework for analyzing implementation aspects of policies and programs*. Report for the Office of the Assistant Secretary for Planning and Evaluation. Washington, DC: Department of Health Education and Welfare.

Siegel, K., & Doty, P. (1978). Advocacy research versus management review: A comparative analysis. *Policy Analysis, 5*, 37-65.

Simmons, O. G., & Saunders, L. (1974). *The present and prospective state of policy approaches to fertility*. Paper presented at the Social Science Research on Population and Development Conference, New York, October.

Smith, A. G., & Robbins, A. E., (1982). Structured ethnography: The study of parental involvement. *American Behavioral Scientist, 26*(1), 45-61.

Smith, A. G., & Seashore-Louis, K. (1982). Multimethod policy research. *American Behavioral Scientist, 26*(1).

Snapper, K., & Seaver, D. (1981). Program decisions: Evaluating a bird in the hand versus two in the bush. *Evaluation and Program Planning, 4,* 325-334.

Stake, R. E. (1983). Stakeholder influence in the evaluation of Cities-In-Schools. In A. S. Bryk (Ed.), *Stakeholder-based evaluation.* San Francisco: Jossey-Bass.

Stewart, D. (1984). *Secondary research: Information sources and methods.* Beverly Hills, CA: Sage.

Stokes, B. (1977, May). *Filling in the family planning gap.* World-Watch Paper No. 12.

Teune, H. (1978). A logic of comparative policy analysis. In D. E. Ashford (Ed.), *Comparing public policies.* Beverly Hills, CA: Sage.

Thompson, M. S. (1980). *Benefit-cost analysis for program evaluation.* Beverly Hills, CA: Sage.

Thompson, M. S., Rothrock, J. K., Strain, R., Palmer, R. H., (1981). Cost analysis for program evaluation. In R. F. Conner, *Methodological advances in evaluation research.* Beverly Hills, CA: Sage.

Tropman, J. E., & McClure, J. K. (1980). Values dualism and social policy affecting the elderly. *Policy Studies Journal, 9*(4), 604-613.

Van de Val, M., & Bocas, C. (1982). Using social policy research for reducing social problems: An empirical analysis of structure and function. *Journal of Applied Behavioral Science, 18*(1), 49-67.

Wade, L. L. (1972). *The elements of public policy.* Columbus, OH: Charles Merrill.

The Washington Post. (1983a). Stockman, on the mend, reeducates Reagan. February 6.

The Washington Post. (1983b). Parents group matures into strong lobby for school funds. February 14.

Watts, H. (1971, May). *Mid-experiment report on basic labor supply response.* Madison, WI: Institute for Research on Poverty.

Weiss, C. H. (1977). Research for policy's sake: The enlightenment function of social research. *Policy Analysis, 3,* 531-545.

Weiss, C. H. (1978). Improving the linkage between social research and public policy. In L. E. Lynn (Ed.), *Knowledge and policy: The uncertain condition.* Washington, DC: National Academy of Sciences.

Wildavsky, A. (1979). *Speaking truth to power: The art and craft of policy analysis.* Boston: Little, Brown.

Woll, P. (1974). *Public policy.* Cambridge, MA: Winthrop.

Yin, R. (1984). *Case studies.* Beverly Hills, CA: Sage.

ABOUT THE AUTHOR

Ann Majchrzak has been actively involved in conducting policy research for several years. As a contract researcher, she has worked with such government offices as the Assistant Secretary for Planning and Evaluation, HHS; Office of Human Development Services, HHS; National Institute of Mental Health; Office of Technology Assessment; U.S. Marine Corps; and the Navy Personnel Research and Development Center. Her policy research studies have ranged from a congressionally mandated study on the implementation of state social service block grants to the development of policy options for managing problem personnel in the military. She has published numerous articles, including a handbook on policy research for the United Nations Fund for Population Activities.

Dr. Majchrzak is Assistant Professor of Organizational Behavior at Purdue University's Krannert Graduate School of Management.